Archer's
Bible
PRESENTS:

# THE BOWHUNTER'S GUIDE

### by Dwight Schuh

Stoeger Publishing Company • Accokeek, Maryland

**Stoeger Publishing.**
*Great Outdoor Books & More Since 1924*

## STOEGER PUBLISHING COMPANY
## is a division of Benelli USA

### Benelli USA
*Vice President and General Manager:*
  Stephen Otway
*Vice President of Marketing and Communications:*
  Stephen McKelvain

### Stoeger Publishing Company
*President:* Jeffrey Reh
*Publisher:* Jay Langston
*Managing Editor:* Harris J. Andrews
*Design & Production Director:*
  Cynthia T. Richardson
*Photography Director:* Alex Bowers
*Imaging Specialist:* William Graves
*National Sales Manager:* Jennifer Thomas
*Special Accounts Manager:* Julie Brownlee
*Credit Manager:* Karen Cushman
*Publishing Assistant:* Shannon Rollins
*Administrative Assistant:* Gennifer Davis
*Design & Layout:* Peggy Archambault
*Proofreader:* Celia Beattie

Published by Stoeger Publishing Company
17603 Indian Head Highway, Suite 200
Accokeek, Maryland 20607

BK0305
ISBN: 0-88317-249-6
Library of Congress Control Number:
  2002110067
Printed in the United States of America.
Distributed to the book trade and
to the sporting goods trade by:
Stoeger Industries
17603 Indian Head Highway, Suite 200
Accokeek, Maryland 20607
301-283-6300   Fax: 301-283-6986
www.stoegerpublishing.com

### OTHER PUBLICATIONS:
**Shooter's Bible**
  The World's Standard Firearms
    Reference Book
**Gun Trader's Guide**
  Complete Fully Illustrated
    Guide to Modern Firearms with
    Current Market Values

### HUNTING & SHOOTING:
Advanced Black Powder Hunting
Archer's Bible
Complete Book of Whitetail Hunting
Cowboy Action Shooting
Elk Hunter's Bible
Great Shooters of the World
High Performance Muzzleloading
  Big Game Rifles
Hounds of the World
Hunt Club Management Guide
Hunting America's Wild Turkey
Hunting and Shooting
  with the Modern Bow
Hunting Whitetails East & West
Hunting the Whitetail Rut
Labrador Retrievers
The Pocket Survival Guide
Shotgunning for Deer
Taxidermy Guide
Tennessee Whitetails
Trailing the Hunter's Moon
The Turkey Hunter's Tool Kit:
  Shooting Savvy
The Ultimate in Rifle Accuracy
Whitetail Strategies

### COLLECTING BOOKS:
The Lore of Spices
Sporting Collectibles
The Working Folding Knife

### FIREARMS:
Antique Guns
Complete Guide to Modern Rifles
Complete Guide to Service Handguns
Firearms Disassembly
  with Exploded Views
FN Browning Armorer to the World
Gunsmithing at Home
Heckler & Koch:
  Armorers of the Free World
How to Buy & Sell Used Guns
Modern Beretta Firearms
Model 1911: Automatic Pistol
Spanish Handguns
The Ultimate in Rifle Accuracy
The Walther Handgun Story

### RELOADING:
Complete Reloading Guide
The Handloader's Manual of
  Cartridge Conversions 3rd Ed.
Modern Sporting Rifle Cartridges

### FISHING:
Bassing Bible
Catfishing: Beyond the Basics
The Complete Book of Flyfishing
Deceiving Trout
Fishing Made Easy
Fishing Online: 1,000 Best Web Sites
The Fly Fisherman's Entomological
  Pattern Book
Flyfishing for Trout A-Z
The Flytier's Companion
The Flytier's Manual
Handbook of Fly Tying
Ultimate Bass Boats

### COOKING GAME:
The Complete Book of
  Dutch Oven Cooking
Dress 'Em Out
Fish & Shellfish Care & Cookery
Game Cookbook
Wild About Freshwater Fish
Wild About Game Birds
Wild About Seafood
Wild About Venison
Wild About Waterfowl
World's Best Catfish Cookbook

### WILDLIFE PHOTOGRAPHY:
Conserving Wild America
Freedom Matters
Wild About Babies

### FICTION:
Wounded Moon

### NONFICTION:
Escape In Iraq:
  The Thomas Hamill Story

### PHOTOGRAPHY CREDITS:
Cover and title page photography by Charles J. Alsheimer

# Contents

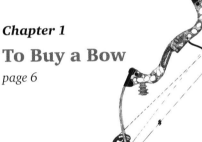

*Introduction*

# The Bowhunting Passion

Maybe you've never shot or hunted with a bow and aren't really convinced that bowhunting is for you. That's an important consideration, because to thrive in bowhunting you must have realistic expectations. If you take up the bow and arrow with the wrong motives, you simply won't last. If you take up bowhunting for the right reasons, you will not only last, but you will develop a passion that you have never experienced in any other outdoor pursuit. Bowhunters are passionate about what they do.

The most obvious reasons are pragmatic. Bow seasons are generally longer than firearms seasons, many take place before firearms seasons when big game moves in their natural patterns, and many fall during the rut. All of these offer great hunting advantages.

Many states have generous archery bag limits, particularly for whitetail deer, and many urban areas limit hunters to bows only, which opens up opportunities for hunting areas that are otherwise off-limits — and often are the range of mammoth bucks.

In general, bow seasons are less crowded, and because bows are quiet, you don't sense the presence of competition, even when the woods are full of other bowhunters. These practical reasons attract many people into bowhunting, because, in a sense, they make hunting easier and more pleasant.

Ironically, a high percentage of people get into bowhunting for a reason that seems to contradict these advantages — challenge. These folks commonly say something like, "Rifle hunting just got too easy. I was looking for more of a challenge." For many of us, challenge is the very reason for bowhunting. A survey sponsored by the National Shooting Sports Foundation asked people why they got into bowhunting. Fifty-eight percent of respondents listed "challenge," while 24 percent listed "longer seasons," 13 percent "it's less crowded," and 11 percent "the seasons start earlier."

A major aspect of this challenge is getting within bow range of animals, often 20 yards or closer. That kind of proximity really supercharges a bowhunting situation, and hunters who are used to shooting big game at 300 yards with a rifle cannot believe the thrill they experience the first time they find themselves 20 yards from a buck deer or bull elk.

While close-range intensity is the drug that hooks most bowhunters, other advantages sink the hook deeper. For one, you can shoot your bow year around. In winter, clubs and shops hold indoor leagues, and in spring and summer they conduct 3-D tournaments and trail shoots. And you can practice just about anywhere, including your backyard or basement. Try that with a .300 magnum. Also, try watching the bullets fly from a .300 magnum. Most die-hard archers will say, "I just love watching arrows fly."

Archery has a personal appeal, because your body and mind are integral to shooting the bow. Imparting your own power into an energy-storing device, releasing the stored energy, and watching the result — an arrow speeding to the target — is captivating.

Bowhunting also offers social interaction. Most towns of any size have archery clubs, and bowhunters gather at banquets and tournaments to enjoy fellowship. On a couple of occasions, I have participated in a hunt sponsored by the Christian Bowhunters of America at Tar Hollow State Forest in Ohio. It's a great gathering of wonderful people and turns out to be a lot of fun. Conversely, I've hunted elk for 14 days without seeing so much as another human being, which I consider to be rewarding and stimulating. Maybe that's another irony of bowhunting — while bowhunters are the most reclusive of individuals, they can also be some of the most social.

Finally, archery and bowhunting have a rich history. For many, bowhunting is a tradition, part of the fabric of the continuum of history. The bow has been used for thousands of years in hunting, fighting, and competition. Even in North America the tradition runs deep, from Native American bows and arrows to the exploits of Maurice and Will Thompson to Doug Easton, Fred Bear, and countless others.

All of these qualities build an unquenchable passion in the hearts of bowhunters. My bowhunting passion began in 1969, right after I'd served three years in the U.S. Army. I was 24 years old, independent, and had time on my hands. When a friend invited me to go bowhunting with him, I figured why not? I had nothing better to do, and it was a good way to kill some time until college classes started in the fall.

Up until that point, my real passion had always been duck hunting. But after practicing shooting a longbow all summer, I learned to love the sight of arrows in flight, and the challenge of placing those arrows in a bull's-eye captivated me.

Then, on opening morning of the archery season in eastern Oregon, I marveled at the beauty and peace of the scene. Even though I saw other hunters, it was as if they were not there. And I saw more big bucks than I'd seen in several years of off-and-on rifle hunting. From that moment, my interest in bowhunting exploded into a full-blown passion.

In more than 30 years since, the passion and challenge have never diminished. Getting within bow range always remains difficult and never guarantees an animal in the bag. Developing shooting skills with the bow takes hours of practice, and putting those skills to work on a deer takes iron nerves.

The variety of game available to bowhunters further generates lifetime interest. After hunting deer for several years, I began to think about new opportunities. At first I expanded to elk in my home state of Oregon. Then I began to travel out of state to hunt elk, mule deer, and whitetails.

Since that early beginning, I have pursued whitetails in the big forests of the Pacific Northwest, the farmlands and woodlots of the Midwest, the hardwood bottoms and pine plantations of the Deep South; sheep and mountain goats in the highest peaks of the West and Far North; elk, mule deer, and black bear throughout 11 western states and several Canadian provinces; moose in the Lower 48, Canada, and Alaska. At this writing, I have taken 22 species of North American big game from Alaska to Mexico, Alabama to California, as well as five species in South Africa. That kind of variety assures modern bowhunters infinite new horizons to conquer, endless challenges to pursue.

For my first 10 years of bowhunting, I shot recurve bows and longbows, and have continued to hunt with traditional bows since that time. In 1979, I hunted for the first time with a compound bow, and since then I have set up, tuned, and hunted with 50 or more compound bows of various brands and styles. The variety and challenge of the equipment is enough in itself to keep the passion burning strong.

Everything you read in this book is drawn from my bowhunting background. It is a compilation of the knowledge and experience I've gained from many years of bowhunting many different species under a broad range of conditions, with a variety of tackle, shooting styles, and hunting methods.

This book is not written as a graduate course on big game hunting with bow and arrow. It is intended as a foundation and guide to successful bowhunting. If I have learned nothing else in my 30-something years of bowhunting, it is that a solid foundation and good fundamentals are the basis for bowhunting passion and success. My one hope would be that you attain those qualities through this book.

Enjoy your bowhunting.


Dwight Schuh

*Chapter 1*

# To Buy a Bow

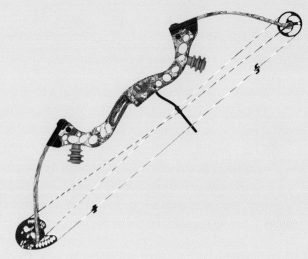

As a boy, I had an inexpensive Bear bow, made from one solid piece of wood, with curved tips, often called static recurve tips. No one showed me how to shoot that bow, so my shooting efforts were crude. I never hunted with that bow, so I created no fond memories from the field with the bow. And I never shot in any tournaments, so my pride hardly came from winning any prizes.

Nonetheless, the bow fascinated me, and I shot it for hours on end, simply because I loved to watch arrows fly through the air. Even today I clearly remember the excitement I felt at watching the flight of the arrow.

Not only do I remember my fascination from years ago, but even today, 50 years later, I still enjoy that same fascination as arrows fly from my bow into a target. My bows today are far more sophisticated, and my knowledge and shooting ability are much greater. But the beauty of arrows in flight has not changed, and I suspect you will feel the same as you start launching arrows from a bow.

*During my first 10 years of bowhunting, I shot recurve bows. This photo was taken on a black-tail deer hunt in California in 1977, when I was shooting a 57-pound Kittredge (Howatt) recurve.*

# Choosing a Bow

Fifty years ago the arrow-launching options were limited to rudimentary recurve bows and longbows. The options are much greater today, but the end result is the same, so it's just a question of how you want to get there.

First, do you want to shoot traditional bows or compounds — or both? Traditional bows would generally be defined as longbows and recurves. A lot of bowhunters broadly call these stickbows. Compounds are any bows that use a system of cables and eccentric wheels or cams to "compound" the energy of the bow. Most of these today are simple two-wheel bows, although there are variations, such as the Oneida, which does not have wheels on the limb tips but rather cams inside the riser (handle) of the bow.

In the 1970s, when compound bows began to gain in popularity, most bowhunters started out with a recurve or longbow and then "graduated" to a compound. Today that trend has flip-flopped and most people start with a compound and then "graduate" into a stickbow.

My personal journey is fairly typical. I shot my traditional Bear bow for several years until one of the limb tips got slammed in a car door. That probably didn't affect my archery career a lot, because that's about the time I started high school, when my interests switched from watching arrows to watching skirts. But after graduating from high school and college and getting married, the arrow watching again took priority.

I borrowed a friend's longbow to hunt with one year and loved every minute of it. I bought myself a new 48-pound Wing Thunderbird recurve and a couple of years later a 57-pound Kittredge (Howatt) recurve and hunted with these for 10 years.

*In 1979 I hunted for the first time with a compound bow, and in 1980 I took this Nevada mule deer with a Jennings T-Star, Easton aluminum 2216 arrow, and Zwickey broadhead.*

About 1980, tendinitis in my shoulders got so severe that I started dabbling for the first time with a compound to see if I could shoot with less pain. It helped, and I shot and hunted almost exclusively with compounds for the next 20 years. But in recent years, as my shoulders have recovered and I look for new challenges, my love affair with recurves and longbows has been revived, and now I own several stickbows and shoot and hunt with them regularly.

Many hunters undergo a similar evolution.

## Starter Bows

Given my background, and judging from the experience of many other bowhunters, I recommend that you start with a compound bow. The reasons are numerous:

- Draw weight is adjustable, allowing you to start out at a low draw weight for learning and increase the draw weight as you grow in experience and strength.
- Peak weight at mid-draw drops off to about one-third of the weight at full draw. Thus, with a 60-pound bow compound you're holding roughly 20 pounds at full draw. Reduced holding weight takes the strain off your muscles and allows you to concentrate strictly on form and aiming.

- Most compound bows are equipped with sights. You will gain pinpoint accuracy much faster shooting with sights than shooting without sights (barebow) as most stickbow shooters do.
- Compound bows are cut to center (that is, the sight window is recessed so that a nocked arrow sits directly in line with the path of the bowstring), and they are equipped with adjustable arrow rests. These qualities make them easy to tune, so that you can achieve nearly perfect arrow flight quickly and easily. That's not always the case with stickbows.
- A compound bow stores — and thus delivers — considerably more energy than the average traditional bow of equal draw weight. Thus, you can shoot a lighter compound while gaining flatter arrow trajectory and greater potential penetration on big game animals.

All of these collectively translate into fun, confidence, and success. While these qualities are valuable for all of us, they're particularly appealing for young people and ladies who might not be as driven as some men, and who might struggle to shoot a stickbow of hunting weight. With a lightweight compound just about anybody can be hitting targets regularly and hunting efficiently within a few weeks.

Having said this, why would anyone choose traditional tackle? The reasons are many. The simplicity and beauty of recurves and longbows are appealing, and the act of drawing a bow and feeling the full weight that launches the arrow yields a satisfaction that's lacking in shooting a high-letoff compound.

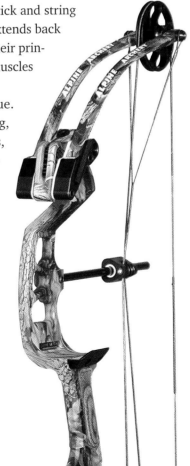

*The Alpine Ravage below shows typical features that make modern compounds easy to tune and shoot. The sight window cut well past center assures easy, center-line tuning and total arrow clearance past the riser. Split limbs, single cam, synthetic cable and string, and pivoting limb pockets are all modern features that enhance performance.*

The history of traditional bows is rich. With a simple stick and string in hand, you sense the historical power of archery that extends back centuries. While modern stickbows are truly high-tech, their principle is ancient, and you feel that antiquity when your muscles bend the limbs to launch an arrow. It's a good feeling.

Along with that comes an entire traditional mystique. Most traditionalists go beyond target practice, hunting, and history and delve into making their own arrows, strings, quivers, and bows. And therein is the fascination. Many a traditionalist has killed a wild turkey with his bow and then used the wing feathers to fletch a batch of custom cedar arrows stained and painted to reflect the hunt on which he is taking those arrows. It's not only hands-on, but it's very personal. Sitting in a shop amid fragrant cedar shavings, crafting an arrow, bow, or other gear goes far beyond the practical. It's an art, a product of the heart.

The physical qualities of stickbows are appealing. Whether it is a featherweight longbow weighing less than a pound or a more blocky recurve weighing 3 pounds, a traditional bow is a joy to carry in the field compared to the mechanical heft of a compound bow. And the simplicity is equally appealing. You literally have a stick and string, so little can go wrong. If you work at it, you might break a bow limb or cut the string, but that's about it. Compared with the mechanical complication of compounds, the simplicity of traditional bows appeals to many people.

Then comes challenge — one of the most commonly stated reasons for switching from a compound to a stickbow. After a few years of shooting a compound, hitting the bull's-eye or killing a deer at 20 yards might seem too routine, too assured for some people, and they crave more challenge. So they switch to traditional archery. Simply getting the arrows to fly straight can be a challenge, and perfecting accuracy demands a whole new level of commitment. For some bowhunters, that's reason enough to shoot a stickbow.

*Many traditionalists argue that bowhunting is meant to be a close-range sport, and that's the very reason for shooting a traditional bow. While still-hunting, Doug Chase took this Oregon blacktail buck at a range of 20 yards.*

Average maximum effective range for most people shooting compounds is probably somewhere around 40 yards. For most people shooting stickbows it's closer to 20. While this could be a strong argument for shooting a compound, avid traditionalists will argue that it's good reason — the reason — to shoot a stickbow. It forces you to hunt better and get closer. That's good, they would argue, because bowhunting is meant to be a close-range sport. And there's a lot of truth in that.

Finally, some people would argue that stickbows are more effective hunting tools because they can be shot quickly and fluidly from all positions. While I love to shoot and hunt with stickbows, I would be hard pressed to agree with this view. It is true that you can crouch and shoot under limbs or around a tree trunk or boulder, feats that would be difficult or impossible with a sighted compound, which must be held vertically. However, in most situations the pinpoint accuracy, the light holding weight (which allows you to hold longer in tense situations), and the short, maneuverable length all make compounds generally more efficient for hunting.

Statistics should bear this out. During the 1999-2000 biennial recording period, hunters entered 4,177 whitetail deer in the Pope & Young record book. Of these, 90 percent were taken with compound bows. Of 258 mule deer entered during the same period, 93 percent were taken with compound bows. Similar percentages hold for most other species. If traditional bows were truly more effective, a higher percentage of animals would be taken with them.

Bottom line is that there are different reasons for shooting compound and traditional bows, but they're all valid. Again, for starting out and learning the basics of bowhunting, I recommend a compound. But as you grow in the sport, seek greater challenges, and crave to delve more into the history and mystique of archery and bowhunting, you will simply be drawn to traditional tackle. You probably won't be able to help yourself.

## Eye Dominance

Regardless of your choice of tackle, the most fundamental decision is whether to shoot right- or left-handed. You might think this depends on hand dominance, but that's not true. It really depends on eye dominance. And the two are not always the same.

To determine eye dominance, keep both eyes open and point with your index finger at a distant object, say a power pole across the street. Now close your left eye. If your finger still appears to be pointing directly at the pole, your right eye is dominant. If, however, your finger appears to be pointing to the right of the pole, you probably have a dominant left eye. To double-check this, start again with both eyes open. Now close your right eye. If, while looking with only your left eye, your finger appears to be pointing directly at the pole, you clearly have a dominant left eye.

Accepted wisdom says you should shoot on the side of your dominant eye, regardless of hand dominance, and I believe that's right. A friend of mine, who is right-handed, was having a terrible time aiming his bow. He just seemed confused. Checking his eye dominance, we discovered he had a strongly dominant left eye. We switched him to a left-handed bow, and his shooting improved instantly and dramatically. A number of prominent archers, among them Jim Dougherty and Glenn Helgeland, are right handed but shoot left-handed bows for this reason.

Thus, I would advise you to shoot on the side of your dominant eye. It will make aiming much easier, especially if you shoot without sights. In that scenario, you just about have to shoot with both eyes open, which forces you to aim with the dominant eye. If you shoot with sights, you can get away with shooting on the side of your weaker eye by closing the dominant eye while aiming. That's a workable solution. Still, overall, you'll shoot more naturally and comfortably if you aim with your dominant eye.

## Choosing a Compound Bow

Draw length is one of the few subjects in archery that won't rouse a lot of debate, because physical stature determines

*When this man points at the chimney with both eyes open, his finger appears to be pointing directly at the chimney. If he then closes his left eye and his finger still appears to be pointing at the chimney, he has a dominant right eye.*

*If he closes his right eye and looks only with his left, his finger will appear to be pointing to the right of the chimney, further confirming that his right eye is dominant.*

*You can get a rough idea of draw length by holding a yardstick against your upper chest and extending your fingertips as far as possible along the yardstick. This man has a draw length of roughly 27½ inches.*

draw length, and no one can change that. A grade-schooler or a small lady might have a draw length of 24 inches, while a large man might have a draw length of 32 inches. And this measurement is critical, because it affects both shooting comfort and accuracy. That's why, in choosing a compound bow, one size does not fit all and picking up a cheap bow at a garage sale is rarely a good deal. Your money is far more wisely spent at a pro shop where you will get a bow fit to your build.

The Archery Manufacturers and Merchants Organization (AMO) defines draw length as true draw plus 1¾ inches. Thus, to determine your AMO draw length you must first determine your true draw, which is the distance from the nocking point on the bow string to the low point of the grip on the bow at full draw.

You can get a good idea of your draw length by placing a yardstick against your chest just below your throat and extending your fingertips out along the yardstick as far as you can reach. If you can reach 28¼ inches along the yardstick, then your true draw is about 28¼ inches. In buying a compound bow, you would add 1¾ inches to that. Thus, you would buy a compound bow with a draw length of 30 inches.

Perhaps a more accurate way to measure draw length is to pull a bow and measure your draw length at full draw. But this is best done with a light traditional bow. Why? As my good friend and archery coach Dave Holt points out, a compound bow has a set draw length. If you pull a compound, you will simply adjust your body to the pre-set draw length of the bow. Thus, you end up measuring the bow's draw length, not your draw length.

In contrast, a traditional bow has no set draw length. So with it you pull the string to a comfortable distance for you, which gives you a true measure of your draw, not the bow's. Why a light traditional bow? Because, if you draw a hunting weight stickbow, you will probably strain to reach full draw and may not get a measurement of your true draw length. With a bow lighter than 30 pounds draw weight, you should have no problem easily drawing to your true draw length.

Here's another way to determine AMO draw length: With a friend standing by, nock an arrow and draw the bow to a comfortable point. If you're drawing with your fingers, anchor by placing the tip of your index finger in the corner of your mouth. Keep the elbow of your bow arm slightly bent. Now have your friend make a mark with a felt-tip pen on the arrow directly above the low point in the grip (that is, where your hand presses against the bow).

Now let down and measure the arrow from the low point in the nock to the pen mark on the shaft. That distance is your true draw length. To get your AMO draw length, add 1¾ inches. Again, if your true draw is 28¼ inches, your AMO draw length computes to 30 inches, and you will order a compound bow with a draw-length rating of 30 inches.

This is a good starting point, but it's not carved in stone. As you shoot and gain strength, your draw length could increase slightly. Also, your AMO draw length depends on your shooting method. If you start out shooting with fingers' and then switch to a release aid, you'll probably need to shorten the draw length of your bow slightly, because the head of the release extends forward of your fingers anchor point. Adding a string loop will shorten the draw length of your bow another half-inch or so.

One last thought on draw length: You will shoot best if you keep draw length slightly on the short side. Some people strain to make their draw length as long as possible, with their bow arms as straight and stiff as broomsticks and their heads tipped back so they can see through their peep sights. They demonstrate exactly how not to shoot. It is far better to keep your bow arm relaxed and slightly bent at the elbow, and your head in a relaxed, natural position when you're at full draw. Again, if you err one way or the other, err on the short side, not the long side. You'll shoot better.

Let's consider draw weight. A friend of mine showed me a videotape of a man on a bear stand. When a bear came to the bait, the hunter tried to draw his bow, but could not break-over his bow, even by raising the bow over his head. Finally, as he struggled to draw, his arrow fell to the ground. He failed four times before managing, with a mighty effort, to reach full draw.

The hunter was grossly over-bowed, and for what purpose? The fact is, you should be able to draw your bow smoothly and easily under hunting conditions. Yes, the heavier the draw weight, generally the faster the arrow speed. But you hardly need an arrow shooting 300 feet per second (fps) when you're shooting whitetails at 20 yards and closer.

Before accurate rangefinders, high arrow speed and flat trajectory had some value. But the advent of laser rangefinders has virtually devalued the need for ultrafast bows. You're far better off shooting a bow at a "slow" 250 fps easily and accurately than straining to shoot a scorcher at 300 fps.

How do you gauge reasonable draw weight? Initially, sit flat on the floor and draw your bow. If you have to strain or raise it over your head to reach full draw, the bow is too heavy for you. Lower the draw weight until you can pull smoothly and without strain.

In the field you should be able to hold your bow in shooting position, with your sight on the target, and draw straight back, slowly and smoothly, without raising your bow or quivering to reach full draw. Then, when an animal approaches within bow range, you can draw with little movement — only the elbow of your drawing arm creeps back — to reach full draw.

Just remember that backyard conditions usually differ greatly from hunting conditions. Drawing your bow may be easy in practice, but it could be a whole different story after you've been freezing on stand for hours or have crawled for miles on a long stalk.

Years back I stalked a whitetail buck on the plains of Colorado. He was bedded next to a fence clogged with tumbleweeds. After I'd spent a couple of hours circling around and crawling to get within range of the buck, he got up and followed a doe down the fence toward me. When he came within 20 yards I started to draw — but could not. And this was with a bow I could draw easily in practice. My shoulders and arms were so fatigued from crawling and tension that they would not work. The buck walked away, none the worse for his close call.

You might ask: How much draw weight do I need to be effective? It's impossible to prescribe a precise level for every situation, because the variables are so great. But based on my own experience, observations of dozens of kills by other hunters, and stories from dozens of other hunters, I would say a modern compound bow of 40 pounds draw weight is adequate for deer, black bears, antelope, and other game of similar size. For elk, moose, caribou, and other large animals, 50 pounds would be a more realistic minimum. For stickbows, you would need to add about 10 pounds to those minimums. If you can easily draw and shoot heavier weights, all the better. Shoot as heavy as you can handle. However, I would say that a modern 60-pound compound is more than adequate for any big game in North America.

## Cam Style

Cam style has evolved over the years from the four- and even six-wheel designs of the 1970s to the standard two-wheel, single-cam bows of today. Matt McPherson's Solo Cam, first introduced in the early 1990s, did not catch on instantly, because some people perceived it as slower than the radical two-cam bows. Also, they said, the long bowstring required by the single cam, over 100 inches in some cases, would stretch and alter the bow's performance.

But the single-cam concept has been refined to such an extent that single cams now are as hot as any two-cam bows, and modern string materials have virtually eliminated problems with stretching strings. To put it another way, single-cam bows are generally considered the best choice for bowhunters today, and most bow manufacturers report that single-cam bows comprise about 80 percent of their sales.

Let me explain. With two-cam bows, the wheels work in harmony, and they must be synchronized for best performance. That is, when the string is released they must roll over at precisely the same time. If they do not, they will jerk the string — thus the nocking point and the arrow — up and down. If synchronization is off by far, arrow flight can be erratic at best.

About 1990 I took part in a high-speed filming project done by Easton. A number of archers shot arrows in front of a camera that filmed at the speed of 7,000 frames per second. Needless to say, that produced some very slow-motion views of our arrows in flight. We learned a number of things from this project, but one of the most remarkable was to see the effects of poor cam synchronization. On some of the bows, the nocking point jerked violently up and down several times as it drove the arrow forward. The result was that the arrow was flapping like a porpoise tail by the time it cleared the rest. For die-hard archers who have the know-how and equipment to synchronize the cams, this is no big problem. But that doesn't describe the average bowhunter. Most bowhunters will never do that, so they just settle for mediocre arrow flight and accuracy.

Enter the single-cam bow, which has a large cam on the bottom limb and an idler wheel on the top. With only one cam, there is nothing to synchronize. Thus, the bow cannot go out of "tune." This fact makes the single-cam bow a boon to modern bowhunters. In addition, single-cam bows generally seem to be smoother to draw and quieter to shoot. The quiet aspect may be a result of other silencing additions, but the cam design itself seems to produce less of a "whap" sound as the bow is fired.

Hybrid systems such as the Darton CPS (Controlled Power System) and the Hoyt Cam & ½ employ a standard high-energy cam on the bottom limb, but they have a cam-shaped "idler" wheel on the top limb. The off-round upper wheel allows the use of two cables and a standard length bowstring. According to the manufacturers, it controls forward motion of the string better than does a standard single cam with a round idler wheel. Thus, the nock travels straight forward and assures straight-flying arrows right off the rest.

## Bow Length and Weight

Bow length is measured from the axle of the top limb to the axle of the bottom. Thus, any reference here to bow length is axle-to-axle length. Most early compound bows were 46 to 48 inches long, and all of us recurve shooters at the time thought, "No way. That's too radical. Those short little bows will never shoot." Little did we know of the future. If we could have seen one of the modern 32-inch or shorter bows, we would have scoffed, "Ain't no way those toys will shoot." And how wrong we would have been.

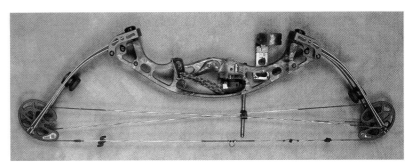

*Hybrid single-cam bows, like the Hoyt CyberTec Cam & ½ shown here, have excellent tuning and shooting characteristics.*

*The upper wheel of Hoyt's Cam & ½ system looks like a cam, but technically it is not, because it does not store energy as the bottom cam does. The upper wheel is designed for straight nock travel and adjustability.*

The release aid is probably most responsible for the development and acceptance of ultra-short bows. When compounds first gained acceptance, some 80 to 90 percent of all archers shot with fingers. They could shoot the compounds of that time just fine with their fingers, but bows under 40 inches were unheard of for finger shooters because finger-pinch became too extreme.

Over time, however, more and more bowhunters have learned the

The release aid has made it possible for modern archers to shoot ultrashort bows accurately. The Buckmaster G2 measures 31 inches, axle to axle.

advantage of the release aid, and today probably 90 percent or more of all compound shooters shoot with release aids. Obviously, the release aid eliminates finger pinching, which opens the door for shorter bows.

Okay, so what is the ideal length for a modern hunting bow? Nobody can dictate the perfect length, because it is subjective to some degree, and it also depends on your size and draw length. For example, if two archers, one with a 24-inch draw length, the other with a 30-inch draw length, are both shooting 36-inch bows, the string angle will obviously be somewhat more acute for the person with the longer draw length.

With that in mind, I'll offer a few opinions. If you're going to shoot a compound with fingers, you probably want to stay with bows of 40 inches or longer. That way the string angle at full draw will be wide enough to give you a clean release.

Even if you shoot with a release aid, I would recommend a bow of 35 inches or longer, at least for starters. Bows shorter than that may be a little hard to shoot accurately, because they can be torqued so easily during the shot. You can always add stability with a stabilizer, but to some extent that defeats the purpose of shooting a short, light bow.

How much should your bow weigh (that is, mass weight, as opposed to draw weight)? If you'll be hunting on foot, say elk hunting where you must hike many miles, the lighter the better. On a Dall sheep hunt in 1997, I took a Diamond bow with a carbon riser. This bow, by itself, weighed 2.9 pounds. Believe me, that light weight was nice during miles of hiking each day. At this writing, High Country Archery makes the lightest bows. All of the High Country "Carbon Tough" bows tip the scales at slightly over 2 pounds. If you're an accomplished archer and want a featherweight bow for off-road hunting, a bow like that is great.

But for average hunting from a tree stand, going to the extremes in light weight and short length is not necessary. A compound in the 35- to 40-inch length range, and weighing a little over 3 pounds is a good starting point.

The Alpine Ravage could be considered ultrashort at 29 inches although, at 4.1 pounds mass weight, it would not be considered ultralight. In choosing a bow, you have to determine which characteristics are most important to you in your style of hunting.

# Letoff

What about letoff? How much do you need? How much is best? First let's see how to determine letoff. The Archery Manufacturers and Merchants Organization (AMO), which sets standards for the archery industry measures letoff as follows:

> "The maximum letoff on a compound bow shall be measured at a point in the draw cycle after the peak draw weight has been attained. It shall be measured near the end of the draw cycle where the minimum holding force is reached. This point in the draw cycle on a compound bow is known as the 'bottom of the valley.'
>
> "Determination of the percent of letoff: The values of peak draw force and the letoff force shall be used to calculate the percent of letoff. The peak force is the maximum force obtained during the draw cycle. The letoff force is the lowest force reached following the peak force during a single uninterrupted draw cycle. In all cases, both the highest and lowest force shall be read from a scale during a single and continual pull condition, without relaxation. This technique eliminates the introduction of hysteresis, which can distort the reading.

$$\frac{(100 \text{ X (PDF) - (MHF)}}{(\text{Peak Draw Force})} = \% \text{ Letoff}$$

Let's say you have a 60-pound bow with 65 percent letoff. To figure the holding weight you would multiply .65 x 60 = 39 pounds. That's the actual amount of letoff. If you subtract 39 pounds from 60, you get 21 pounds of holding weight. A 60-pound bow with 80 percent letoff will give you 48 pounds of letoff and 12 pounds of holding weight.

It might seem that if a little letoff is good, a lot is better, and that's the marketing emphasis used by manufacturers. Thus, the 80 percent letoff compound has become very popular. Again, just as the release aid probably facilitated the evolution of short bows, it also probably facilitated the evolution of high letoff.

That's because, shooting with fingers, you need a certain amount of pressure on your fingers for a clean release. If you're holding only 12 pounds at full draw, you'll have a hard time getting that string to slip off your fingers. For that reason, if you plan to shoot with fingers, you should stick with bows of 65 percent letoff — or lower.

With a release aid, letoff becomes less critical, because, as you trigger the release aid, the string will slip away smoothly, even with very little string tension.

However, high letoff isn't perfect. One problem is that the string has so little tension on it that you can easily torque the string, which could make for inconsistent shooting. Also, keep in mind that in some states, bows with letoff greater than 65 percent are illegal.

A couple of other things to consider are handle shape and brace height. Bows come in three handle shapes — deflexed, straight, and reflexed. On a deflexed bow, the limb pockets lie behind the grip of the handle. On a straight bow, the limb pockets are in line with the grip. On a reflexed bow, the limb pockets lie in front of the handle.

Generally accepted wisdom says that strongly reflexed bows shoot the fastest but are more critical to shoot, while deflexed bows are slightly slower but are more stable and forgiving to shoot. Obviously, the straight riser is a compromise between the two.

Why would reflexed bows shoot faster? To understand this, you must understand the term "brace height," the distance between the bow string and the grip of the bow handle. Some bows have a brace height as low as 6 inches, others as high as 10 inches. Here are two truths:

> The lower the brace height, the faster the bow, all other things (draw weight, bow length, arrow weight, draw length, etc.) being equal. That's because, the lower the brace height, the longer the power stroke. For example, if you have a bow with a 30-inch draw length and a 6-inch brace height, the power stroke (the distance the string stays in contact with the arrow) is 24 inches. If you have another bow with a 30-inch draw length and a 10-inch brace height, the power stroke is only 20 inches. The bow with the longer power stroke will shoot faster because the string is in direct contact with the arrow 4 inches farther.

> Reflexed bows generally have lower brace heights than deflexed bows because the limbs are set forward of the handle, which pulls the string closer to the riser. The resultant low brace height is the main reason reflexed bows are faster (again, all else being equal) than deflexed bows.

You might ask: Why not just buy the most strongly reflexed, and thus the fastest, bow? Good question. And the answer is that there's no such thing as a free lunch. You pay for that speed with a critical, unforgiving bow. In other words, it could be hard to shoot accurately.

Again, let me explain. When you release the bowstring, the string does not suddenly stop when it hits the braced position. It continues forward as much as 2 inches. In slow-motion video, this is quite obvious.

Thus, if you're shooting a bow with a 6-inch brace height, the string will come within 4 inches of the handle — and within 4 inches of the arrow rest — on each shot. If you have any kind of overdraw, the string could very well hit the arrow rest.

What this means is that with a brace height of 6 inches, the bowstring is still in contact with the arrow and is still driving the arrow forward as the fletching passes around or through the rest. A bow is much more forgiving if the arrow has left the string before the fletching contacts the arrow rest. Thus, a bow with a higher brace height is generally easier to shoot consistently. The slight sacrifice in speed is worth the gain in accuracy. I would recommend that you stay with a brace height of at least 7 inches.

## Other Considerations

Most modern compounds have various systems for changing draw length and letoff. These features are worth considering, because they allow you to fine-tune draw length to fit you precisely. And if you ever want to sell your bow, you have the option of changing draw length to fit a prospective buyer.

The two most common systems employ either pegs or modules. With the peg system, you simply move the string from one peg to another to shorten or lengthen the string. It's a simple system, but it does have drawbacks. For one thing, if you lengthen the string to lengthen draw length, you also increase draw weight — and vice versa. Also, you need to relax the bow with a bow press to move the string from one peg to the other. With the module system, you install a different module to alter the amount of string wrap around the cam. Most module systems do not alter draw weight, and you can change the modules without relaxing the bow.

Price and brand are always considerations. As far as brand goes, I can't say one is clearly better than another. I have shot Hoyt, Mathews, Martin, Bear, Jennings, Golden Eagle, Bow Tech, Diamond, High Country, Darton, Parker, Oneida, and other brands, and they all have proved accurate and dependable. Perhaps your decision on brand comes down to the feel, looks, and specific features that appeal to you.

All manufacturers offer bows in different price ranges. Do you need the most expensive model to reach your potential? Not at all. Top-end bows have refinements that make them more appealing, but they don't necessarily shoot any better than economy models. If you can afford only a mid-priced bow, buy it. It will do the job.

If you aren't into making decisions, a good option is the "packaged" bow that comes equipped with quiver, sight, arrow rest, peep sight, and arrows. For example, the Parker E-Z draw comes fully outfitted, tuned, and sighted in. Simply slide the peep sight up or down the string to fit your build and shooting style, adjust the sights to bring the arrows dead center on target, and you're ready to hunt. Outfitted packages are an economical and relatively easy way to get started.

Speaking of getting started, for people with small stature and for young archers, look into the many excellent youth and ladies' bows. Virtually every bow company now makes scaled-down, high-performance models for archers with short draw lengths.

Another excellent alternative is the Genesis bow, manufactured by Mathews Archery. This bow has no letoff, so it has no specific draw length. Anyone with a draw length from 15 to 31 inches can shoot it. The Genesis adjusts from 10 to 20 pounds draw weight, and the newer Genesis Pro, a competition-quality bow, adjusts from 15 to 25 pounds. Thus, these bows are ideal for young children just getting started, but they're also good practice bows for accomplished bowhunters. The Genesis and Genesis Pro are great bows for growing families and clubs, because one bow really does fit all.

**Top:** *The PerfXCam from High Country Archery is the ultimate in adjustability. You can change draw length, draw weight, and percent of letoff.*

**Bottom:** *Some companies use modules for altering draw length and letoff. Changing draw-length modules on the BowTech Patriot is simply a matter of removing two screws, switching modules, and replacing the screws. No bow press is needed.*

# In Summary

Okay, all of that might seem pretty complicated. If I could draw up the perfect bow for you, what would it look like? My recommendation assumes you're new to archery. If that's the case, I would suggest a bow meeting the following specs:

- Shoot on the side of your dominant eye
- Comfortable, relaxed draw length with bow arm slightly bent at the elbow
- Single-cam, soft or medium performance (avoid the hottest models until you get some experience)
- Axle-to-axle length of about 36 inches
- Brace height of 7 inches or higher
- Draw weight for women and teens, 35 to 50 pounds; average men, 45 to 60 pounds; strong guys, 55 to 70 pounds.

# Choosing a Traditional Bow

Many of the principles discussed for compound bows apply to stickbows. Certainly the dominant eye principle does. In fact, if you plan to shoot barebow, you virtually have to shoot on the side of your dominant eye.

Ditto draw weight. You must pick a draw weight you can handle easily. Just remember that you probably can't shoot the same draw weight with a stickbow that you can with a compound. If you shoot a 60-pound compound comfortably, you'll probably struggle with a 60-pound stickbow. Most likely you'll have to drop down to 50 to 55 pounds draw weight.

Also, because you're holding peak weight at full draw, the learning curve is much broader with a stickbow. With a high-letoff compound, you can concentrate on aiming and form at full draw. With a stickbow more of your attention is directed toward simply pulling the weight. I strongly recommend that you buy two bows — the heavier bow you will hunt with, and a light model for learning and practice. I have a cheap, 25-pound recurve I practice with regularly, and it's the foundation for any success I have shooting a heavier stickbow. It allows me to shoot virtually infinitely, and I can focus on form and technique, because I'm not fighting the heavy draw weight of a hunting bow. If you buy a three-piece takedown recurve or longbow, you can buy two sets of limbs — light for practice, heavier for hunting.

Draw length isn't an issue with a stickbow, because there is no set draw length. However, draw length should be roughly matched to bow length. Some stickbows tend to "stack" if drawn much beyond 28 inches. Up to that draw length they gain about 2 pounds of draw weight for each 1 inch of draw length. But when drawn beyond that point, some begin to gain 3 to 4 pounds of draw weight for each additional inch of draw length. That makes the bow difficult and uncomfortable to draw. That's stacking. Generally, shorter bows will start stacking at shorter draw lengths. My first bow was a Browning Nomad, which was 52 inches long. At my 30-inch draw that bow looked like a barrel hoop at full draw, and it stacked like crazy. It was much too short for me and was not smooth drawing at my draw length.

As a rough guide, if you have a draw length of 28 inches or shorter, you probably can shoot a recurve of 56 to 60 inches comfortably. But if your draw length is longer than 28 inches, you probably should look at bows longer than 60 inches. They will tend to draw more smoothly for you at the full extent of your draw length. This is not a fast rule, because some shorter bows are designed for a smooth draw out past 28 inches. But in general, bow length and smoothness of draw are related. Given this fact, this discussion applies primarily to recurves since most longbows, as the name implies, are longer than 60 inches.

Here's one other note on draw length: Most people will have a shorter draw length with a stickbow than with a compound. If you draw 30 inches with a compound, you might draw 28 or 29 with a stickbow. It's simply a matter of holding weight and physical strain.

Not all traditional bows are created equal. The most basic are self-wood longbows. The term "self" means a bow is made from one piece of wood, such as yew or osage. Some may have snakeskin or sinew backing, but they have no lamination or modern backing materials.

At the opposite extreme are modern recurves with limbs designed for greatest speed, laminated limbs with fiberglass backing, molded handles, sight windows cut to center, and strings made of Fast Flight or other modern synthetics. Modern recurves are to self-wood longbows what high-tech compounds are to recurves. The gaps between arrow speed and shootability are vast. In terms of performance, modern longbows fall somewhere between self-wood-bows and modern recurves.

If you are just starting out in traditional archery, I strongly suggest you start with a modern recurve rather than a longbow, simply because recurves generally are easier to shoot accurately. They have form-fit handles and shoot relatively fast. And, compared to many longbows, they are fairly easy to shoot accurately.

The main difference is that most recurves have sight windows cut to center. That means the arrow lies in direct line with the travel of the string. Most longbows, however, are not cut to center, which means that a nocked arrow points to the left (for a right-hand shooter) of the string path. As a result, arrows must be spined perfectly to hit where you're looking. And the average longbow, with its non-center-shot handle, magnifies shooter error dramatically. Thus, attaining consistent accuracy with most longbows is harder than it is with most recurves.

Hybrid longbows present a compromise between the two. They have relatively long, straight limbs like any traditional longbow, but their handles are shaped more like that of a recurve, and most have a sight window cut to center.

One rap against longbows has always been hand shock. That is, when the long, straight limbs sweep forward they stop with quite a jolt, and that jolt vibrates through the bow hand. One solution is the reflex/deflex design, which means the handle is deflexed but the limbs are reflexed. This design softens hand shock and increases arrow speed. Most modern recurve and hybrid bows have this design, as do many traditional longbows as well.

Some modern stickbows have a takedown feature. Some three-piece models have removable limbs. The original Fred Bear Take-Down secured the limbs in place with locking brackets, while most other three-piece models used screw-in limb bolts. Many takedown longbows are two-piece models that break down at the handle, either with a slip sleeve or by various hinging methods. Takedown stickbows are excellent for traveling.

*With a stickbow, you probably will shoot 5 to 10 pounds lower draw weight than you will with a compound.*

*Chapter 2*

# Practical Accessories

After reading Chapter 1, you should have just the right bow in hand for you. Now it's time to equip that bow for shooting and hunting. Never take additions to your bow lightly. Your hunting success depends as much on accessories as it does on the bow.

## General Qualities

If you're setting up tackle for hunting — this book assumes you are — the components must be chosen for hunting conditions. Components that might work fine under the relatively sterile conditions of an archery range might be useless under the abuse of hunting. With that in mind, all compo-nents and accessories must meet certain standards.

***Durability:*** One morning, while heading to my antelope blind in the dark, I stepped off a rock and took a header down a rocky slope. Picking myself up, I was happy to find my body and bow all in one piece. However, when I got into the blind and started to nock an arrow, I discovered that my arrow rest, mounted on a

*Hunting conditions have no respect for man or equipment. Above all, choose equipment for durability. If your bow accessories fail you in the backcountry, your hunt is over.*

central spring, was sticking straight out like a pointing dog's tail. My hunt suddenly came to a screeching halt. Maybe I need to learn to walk, but spills are part of hunting, and arrow rests and other gear must hold up under rough treatment. They must be durable.

I have also broken bowsights, quivers, cable slides, and release aids during hunts. Yes, durability is an essential quality in all equipment. And it's especially critical on remote hunts. If you're sitting in a stand on the Back 40 and your bowsight breaks, you can walk back to the house and repair it. If you're 300 miles from civilization in Alaska, you could be facing disaster.

**Dependability:** This closely relates to durability, but it differs, too. It simply means you must be able to count on your gear to perform its duty. One night I was going through the woods on my way to camp, and when I finally arrived I found that several of the arrows were missing from my bowquiver. Limbs apparently had caught the nock ends of the arrows and jerked them from the quiver. That particular quiver did not secure and protect the arrows well enough.

A friend of mine made a long and difficult stalk to get within 25 yards of a big mule deer. In the cold weather the spring-loaded button on his arrow rest had frozen solid, and he shot 2 feet left of the deer. The rest was durable enough, just not dependable in cold weather.

Along similar lines, a rest must hold your arrow securely. If your arrow falls off the rest as you draw during a slight crosswind, you'll lose shot opportunities. The rest must be built to cradle or capture the arrow to hold it securely in place during the entire shot process.

**Adjustability:** Some components, most notably the rest and sight, must be adjusted for accuracy and performance. So these components must be fully and easily adjustable. At the same time, they must be reasonably simple. Some companies have made their micro-adjustable accessories so complicated that they're simply too intricate and heavy for practical hunting use. These are fine for target shooting, but for hunting, the simpler and lighter, the better.

## Arrow Rests

The arrow rest can't really be called an accessory, because it's essential to shooting a bow. Virtually all modern compound bows have handles cut well past center. Thus, these bows must be equipped with arrow rests. You cannot shoot an arrow off the shelf, as you can with most traditional bows.

Today, you have dozens of options, and your choice could be critical. The arrow rest is the last contact between the arrow and the bow, and it can have a major effect on arrow flight and accuracy. This can be easily proved by shooting through paper. Slight adjustments in an arrow rest can significantly alter arrow flight, from tail left to tail right, tail high to tail low (see Chapter 4). Thus, the arrow rest is more than a device simply to hold an arrow in place until you release the string. The arrow rest clearly affects arrow flight and accuracy.

Essentially, rests can be broken into three categories: shoot around, shoot through, and drop away. To understand these terms you have to understand how arrows react at the release of the string. In Chapter 1, I mentioned a slow-motion video project conducted by Easton. This video reveals problems created when the cams on two-cam bows are out of synch, but, in addition, the video clearly demonstrates how arrows oscillate as they're driven forward by the string, and this oscillation governs the style of arrow rest you should use.

**Shoot-around Rests:** Clearly, a fingers-released arrow oscillates radically in a horizontal plane. At the release of the string, the fingers (for a right-handed shooter) force the string to the left. In reaction to this sideways string movement, the center of the arrow bellies to the right, then to the left, then to the right. The arrow looks like a salmon swimming powerfully upstream, wagging from side to side. Arrows well matched to the bow stay in contact with the arrow rest for only about their first 6 inches of forward movement. They then wag to the side, totally clearing the rest. Thus arises the accurate term, "shoot-around" rest.

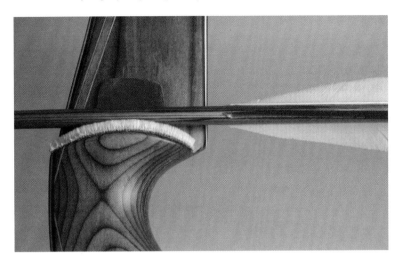

*The bow shelf is the most basic example of the shoot-around arrow rest. Notice how the shelf on this modern Fred Bear Take-Down is curved to minimize contact with the arrow. This shelf is specifically designed to function as an arrow rest.*

The most basic example is the bow shelf, and early bow shelves were just that — shelves — that served as rests more or less by default. They were flat and created a lot of arrow contact, and the result was pretty bad arrow flight. Because of that — this is my interpretation of the situation, which might not be historically correct — many traditional archers started using raised rests to improve arrow flight. With a resurgence of interest in traditional archery today, the emphasis on using the bow shelf as a rest has been revived, and now most bowyers make shelves designed to function as rests. Many modern bow shelves are curved so that the arrow sits on the apex of the curve to minimize arrow contact and improve arrow flight. Most modern traditional bowhunters shoot off the shelf.

One step beyond the bow shelf is the solid raised rest. Early raised rests were made of solid rubber or plastic, and they essentially consisted of a solid, stick-on plate with solid arrow support arm molded into the base. They served the purpose, but they offered no adjustability to improve arrow flight.

From these evolved the flipper/plunger, which consists of a wire support arm coupled with an adjustable, spring-loaded button on the side. The flipper/plunger produced a quantum leap in arrow flight, because flexibility of the support arm and the adjustability of the plunger cushioned the arrow and made the bow/rest setup far more forgiving of shooting errors.

If you shoot a traditional bow with your fingers you will probably shoot off the shelf. For shooting a compound bow with fingers, the flipper/plunger rest like the Plunger Rest from New Archery Products and the Original Arro-Trac from Golden Key-Futura are excellent models.

***Shoot-through Rests:*** Slow-motion video clearly shows that when released with a release aid, the bowstring and thus the arrow react somewhat differently than when released with fingers. Some release aids may push the string slightly to the side, but the most popular styles, such as the caliper, exert no sideways pressure, and the string drives straight ahead at the moment of release, producing little or no horizontal oscillation in the arrow. Rather the arrow oscillates vertically, like a porpoise swimming through the water. On some well-tuned bows, it oscillates very little. Thus, an arrow shot with a release aid will not swing out around the arrow rest. Instead, the shaft stays in contact with the rest its entire length and the fletching slides between, or through, the support arms of the arrow rest. Thus, rests made for use with release aids are appropriately called "shoot-through" rests.

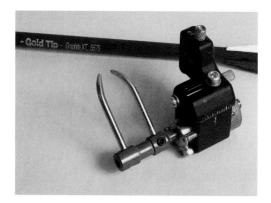

**Right:** *The prong-style rest, such as this Golden Key TM Hunter, has been popular among hunters for a long time. The arrow balances on the two prongs, and vertical tension is adjusted within the body of the rest.*

**Below Right:** *The Golden Key Arrow Trap gives another take on the full-containment concept. It combines a prong-style rest with a bail to prevent the arrow from falling off the rest.*

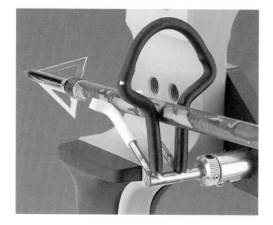

**Bottom Left:** *The Bodoodle at left is a popular blade-style rest. The Savage prong-style rest at right has Teflon prongs for a silent draw.*

**Bottom Right:** *The Whisker Biscuit by Carolina Archery Products, a popular full-containment rest, is an excellent choice for all-around active hunting, because the arrow cannot fall off the rest. Also, concentric pressure on the arrow generally produces excellent arrow flight.*

Prong rests are very popular for hunting. One of the earliest models was the Golden Key-Futura TM Hunter. From this rest, prong-style rests are often generically called "TM" style rests. These rests have two rigid support arms, and the cock vane or feather on the arrow, pointing straight down, slides between the prongs. The prongs themselves are rigid, but vertical spring tension is adjustable. The arrow is more or less balanced on the tips of the prongs. Blade-style rests are similar, but the support arms themselves are flexible, and they're often set at a diagonal tilt to cradle the arrow. Common examples are the Golden Key-Futura Star Hunter, and the various models of Bodoodle rests.

Full-containment rests are a third shoot-through style that has become popular in recent years. The popular Whisker Biscuit is simply a circular brush with a hole in the middle. To nock an arrow, you push it through the hole in the brush. Other styles have three blades that contain the shaft from all sides. The strong point of these rests is that the arrow simply cannot fall off, even in a strong wind, and arrow flight is usually good. One drawback is that these rests can produce a slight hissing sound as you draw and slide the shaft through the rest, which could be a problem at close quarters with a bear or deer on a calm day. You can silence models with flat blades, like the Bodoodle, with moleskin. Because the rests exert pressure equally from all sides, they generally yield excellent arrow flight.

**Drop-away Rests:** The drop-away rest does just what the name suggests — drops away. This concept has been around for decades, but it has been perfected

The Trophy Ridge Dropzone is a solid and reliable drop-away arrow rest. A cord attached to the buss cable pulls the arm up.

and popularized only after the year 2000. When you draw the bowstring, the rest rises into shooting position, raising the arrow with it. Then, when you release, the rest falls out of the way of the arrow, virtually eliminating all contact. On a compound bow, this rest will work for both fingers and release-aid shooters. The Muzzy Zero Effect, Montana Black Gold Trap Door, Trophy Taker, Golden Key-Futura Mirage, and Trophy Ridge are popular fall-away rests. Most of these are raised into position by a cord attached to a cable or the cable slide on the bow, and the support arm is pulled down out of the way by a spring. The Trap Door, an "inertia" rest, has no cord but is cocked into position manually and is triggered to drop down by the release of the string.

Drop-away rests have obvious advantages. While elimination of fletching contact is the most obvious, containment of the arrow shaft is another. Most of these rests have a bail that channels the arrow shaft into a groove at full draw, so the arrow is nearly as secure as it is with a full-containment rest. On the downside, the rests require some tinkering to get just the right setting, and some can be a little noisy as they drop down.

## Bow Sights and String Peeps

The bowsight might not have the essential nature of an arrow rest, because you can shoot any bow without a sight. However, bowsights have become so universal on modern compounds, they could be considered integral, and it's a rare compound archer who doesn't aim with a sight.

**Single-Pin Sights:** Sights can broadly be defined by their setup and purpose. The most basic is the single-fixed-pin sight. This style is ideal for stand hunting in which shot distance is predictable. Probably the most common style would be a single pin set at 20 yards. For any shot closer than that, you simply aim a couple of inches low, and for shots beyond 20 yards, say out to 25, you would place the sight pin slightly above the kill zone. The obvious benefit of this system is simplicity. You never need to worry about choosing the wrong sight pin (always a concern with multiple-pin sights). The obvious drawback is that you're restricted in range. If a buck stands out there at 30 yards or farther, you must hold your sight pin over his back to make a killing shot, which gets a bit imprecise. This system is excellent for situations in which shooting distance is short and predictable — tree stand hunting for whitetails, hunting bears over bait, turkey hunting with decoys at a set distance.

The pendulum (tree stand) sight is a variation on the single-fixed-pin system. Many pendulum sights have a single pin, but the pin swings freely as you tilt your bow at different angles, thus automatically compensating for distance. With most of these sights, you can aim dead on from 0 out to 25 or 30 yards. If you hunt primarily from an elevated stand, the pendulum sight is an excellent choice. About 10 manufacturers make pendulum sights. Look for sturdy construction. Some tend to be a little noisy at the shot.

A third variation on the single-pin concept is the movable sight, such as the Sightmaster. With this sight you move a bracket up or down to adjust the elevation of the sight pin. A calibrated strip on the back of the sight shows the right setting for different yardages. Thus, if you

*The Sightmaster crosshair aperture is good for shooting from a dark blind into the sunlight, as in antelope hunting. This single-pin, adjustable sight is ideal for short, predictable distances.*

have a shot at 20 yards, you adjust the sight to the 20-yard mark. If you have a shot at 50 yards, you adjust to the 50-yard setting. The real strength of this sight is that you always place your sight pin dead-on the target, regardless of distance. Some serious hunters swear by this method, whether they're tree stand hunting at close range or stalking western game where yardages could vary greatly. The obvious shortcoming is that you must adjust the sight prior to the shot, and if you forget to make the adjustment, or you pick the wrong setting the results won't be good. Still, the adjustable, single-pin sight is popular with many serious bowhunters.

**Multiple-Pin Sights:** While single-pin sights may prevail among stand hunters, multiple-pin sights generally dominate among western hunters who hunt on foot. When stalking mule deer, calling in elk, or waiting for antelope at a prairie water hole, your shots could vary from 10 to 50 yards. For these conditions most hunters prefer multiple-pin sights, with each sight pin set for a specific yardage. You can set the pins for any yardages you prefer, and you can add as many pins as you want. I have seen guys with a half-dozen to 10 sight pins on their bows, from 10 to 100 yards. Personally, I think that's overkill. I keep my sights as simple as possible, using four pins set at yardages of 20, 30, 40, and 50 yards, with alternating pin colors of orange, chartreuse, and yellow. This simple system is quick to use under all conditions.

The obvious value of the multiple-pin sight is that you have pin settings for several distances, so you have to make no adjustments prior to the shot. The drawback is that during the heat of the moment you can get confused and aim with the wrong sight pin (I know from experience), and at intermediate distances, you have to hold over or under. However, this does not hamper accuracy significantly. For 35 yards, for example, you simply bracket the kill zone between the 30- and 40-yard pins, and you're right on.

Any multiple-pin sight must have a solid pin guard around the pins to protect them from damage. Most sights using fiber optics have clear pin guards to allow more light to hit the sight

*The Fletcher Tru-Peep hunter with an aperture of about ³⁄₃₂ inch is excellent for hunting. However, with a "free floating" peep like this, you must train your string to bring the peep back at just the right angle for maximum visibility. The sliding knots above and below the peep allow you to move the peep up and down the string as needed.*

pins. Just make sure the pin guard is strong. Some sights screw directly to the side of the bow, and others have a dovetail mounting system. If you travel a lot and want to remove the sight from your bow for packing, the dovetail is handy. Otherwise, a solid mount is fine.

Gang adjustment, which allows you to move all sight pins at one time, is always convenient. That way, if you tweak your string or rest and, as a result, change the point of impact of your arrows, you can simply move the entire sight bar to bring the arrows back onto target at all distances. That's a lot simpler than moving sight pins individually.

**Pin Styles:** In the past, sight pins were made of brass or steel, and the size of the ball on the end varied greatly in size from tiny to bulky. Many hunters painted these sight pins various shades of fluorescent colors to enhance visibility. Metal sight pins still exist, but they have been largely replaced by fiberoptic sight pins, which show up better in dim light. Fiberoptic pins work especially well in shadowed woods for whitetails, elk, and other deep-woods animals. I personally use fiberoptic pins for most of my hunting.

However, fiberoptic pins do have shortcomings. The optical fibers themselves are fragile, and some sight makers do nothing to protect the fibers. They simply loop the fibers along the backs of the pins. Going through heavy brush, you are almost guaranteed to rip the fibers off your sight pins. Not good. Also, these fibers melt, so you must keep them away from heat. One time I was standing by a warming fire with my bow in my hand and, in taking a shot later discovered that all the fiber optics had melted off my sight.

Thus, look for models that in some way protect the fibers. The Archer's Choice Big Buck sight has heavyweight fibers wrapped around the steel sight pins. On the Trophy Ridge Matrix, the fiber optics are encased in clear plastic tubing and wrapped around the pin guard for protection. Both of these systems prove to be fairly durable.

Finally, fiber optics do not work well when you're in a dark position aiming toward a target in bright light. For example, in hunting antelope from a dark pit blind, I have found that the sight pins appear black, making aiming difficult on a sunlit antelope. In this situation, I prefer a crosshair sight with black crosswires. With this sight the vertical and horizontal wires show up clearly against a sunlit target, giving a very positive aiming reference point. Unfortunately, with the advent of fiberoptic sight pins, crosshair sights have nearly disappeared from the market. Sightmaster still makes a crosshair aperture, which is good for shooting from a dark blind.

**Top:** *The five-pin sight like this Big Buck from Archer's Choice is a good all-around hunting sight. A stout pin guard is essential on any pin sight.*

**Bottom:** *The Trophy Ridge Matrix fiberoptic sight employs vertical, in-line sight pins, which will not cover the kill zone as you're aiming.*

Other options for making sights more visible are battery-powered lights that mount above the sight pins and can be turned on in dusky situations. Before choosing this option, make sure electronic attachments on the bow are legal in your state. In some states they are not. Also, be aware that the Pope & Young club will not accept animals into its record book if those animals were taken with the aid of electronic devices. Some sight pins are made with tritium aiming dots. These tritium pins can be "charged" with direct light, say from a flashlight, so they glow in dim light. These sights, also, are illegal in some states. For example, the big game regulations in Idaho state: "No person shall take big game animals: With any electronic or tritium-powered device attached to an arrow or bow."

**_Peep Sights:_** Back about 1985, I sneaked within 30 yards of a great mule deer. This buck was in the bag. But when I shot, my arrow hit well to the left of the deer. At first I was flabbergasted, but in thinking back over the shot I realized I probably had not aligned the bow string properly with my aiming eye. As most bowhunters did at the time, I sighted by aligning the string alongside the pupil of my aiming eye. That worked fine as long as everything lined up correctly. But, as my miss demonstrated, that didn't always happen.

Enter the peep sight. The peep is equivalent to the rear sight on a rifle, and the major advantage is positive alignment with the front sight. Without a peep you easily can hold the string a little left or right — as I did on that mule deer — producing hits well to the left or right of the target.

Looking through a string peep, your eye automatically centers the front sight in the peep and virtually guarantees correct sight alignment. That's the value of a peep sight, and nowadays virtually all serious compound shooters use a peep of some kind.

Like all other good things, peep sights have their downside. Reduced visibility of the front sight in dim light is one. Also, a peep can get plugged with water (during a rainstorm) or debris. To prevent these problems, you want to use a peep with a fairly large hole. The minimum should be about $\frac{1}{16}$ inch, and many hunters drill out the aperture to as large as $\frac{1}{8}$ inch. My favorite peep, the Fletcher Tru-Peep, has an aperture of about $\frac{3}{32}$ inch, and I find that just about right for most hunting situations.

With a "free-floating" peep like the Tru-Peep, another potential problem is improper rotation, which prevents your seeing through the peep at full draw. "Free floating" means the peep has no alignment mechanism but is strictly at the mercy of the rotation of the string. With this kind of peep, you have to "train" the string and peep to come back just so. I like this style of peep because it's simple and adds little weight to the string. And once it's trained, it's very reliable.

If you don't want to bother training a peep, try a self-aligning peep. The Fine-Line Zero Peep, for example, has a rubber tube extending from the peep to one of the bow cables. At full draw the tubing stretches to turn the peep at the right angle every time. Drawbacks are that the tubing can deteriorate and break (possibly at an inopportune time), and the tubing makes a slight slapping sound. The Fine-Line Sta Brite has an aperture of $\frac{1}{4}$ inch, and the Pick-A-Peep allows you to pick any one of seven apertures to match the conditions.

The aligning nock set, like the T.R.U. Speed Nok with Peep Aligner and the Tru-Fire Five Star Center Nock, has a little blade that slips inside the nock of the arrow to hold the string — and, thus, the peep — in proper alignment. A well-tied string loop helps to do the same thing.

The Sure Vision Peep is another concept. This is what I call a "horizontal" peep, in that it sits horizontally in the bowstring when the bow is at rest. But as you draw the string, the peep tilts so you can see through the aperture. This style works best on short bows that have an acute string angle.

One other peep-sight concept is called the No Peep, made by Timberline Archery Products. This is an optical device that mounts below the bow sight and eliminates the need for a peep altogether. Rather than looking through an aperture, as you do on a standard peep, you glance at the No Peep to align a dark dot inside a circle. When these are aligned correctly, and your sight pin is on target, you're ready to shoot. It works well in low light, and it helps reveal shooting flaws. So it's a good training device as well as an accuracy aid.

*The Fine-Line Zero Peep has a self-aligning rubber tube that attaches to a bow cable. As you draw, the tube stretches tight and turns the peep sight at the correct angle every shot. Dr. Bob Speegle finds that this system works well for him in hunting conditions.*

## Release Methods

In recent years, probably 90 percent or more of compound shooters use a release aid, so the release aid must be considered integral to modern bowhunting.

**Attachment Method:** Release aids attach to the string in several ways. The style most commonly used by hunters is the caliper style, which has two opposing jaws that close around the string. Other styles have a sear that cocks over the string from one side. Still others are simply a hook that catches the string at an angle and then releases the string as the release aid is rotated.

Some release aids attach directly to the bowstring or to a string loop tied into the bowstring. However, others have a rope attached directly to the release aid itself, and the rope wraps around the bowstring and hooks into the mechanism. Many hunters prefer to remove the rope from the release aid. They then tie a rope loop directly onto the bowstring and attach the release aid onto the string loop.

**Holding Method:** For hunting, probably the most popular attachment method is the wrist strap. You buckle a strap around your wrist and hold the head of the release aid in your hand. The advantage is that all the pulling pressure is against your wrist rather than your fingers. Also, with the release aid strapped to your wrist you're unlikely to lose it. Other models are shaped like a T and are held with three fingers. Still others have a molded handle that is gripped in the palm of the hand.

**Release Method:** Among hunters, the finger-trigger release is probably most popular because it's very simple to use. Essentially you push the trigger forward to close the caliper jaws around the string and then pull the trigger just as you would a rifle trigger to open the jaws and release the string. Most of these do not have a mechanical safety. Your safety is to hold your finger behind the trigger until you're ready to shoot. This is the most natural style of release aid for many people because you're using your index finger and triggering it much like a rifle. That's good up to a point. However, because of the sensitivity of the index finger, you can respond quickly to the trigger and can easily develop a trigger punching or target panic problem with this style of release. Other styles are triggered with the little finger, some with the thumb.

Another type is the back-tension release aid. This model has no triggering mechanism. Rather this is a T style held with the fingers, and it is basically a solid hook. To draw the bow you pull primarily with your index finger. When you're ready to release you begin pulling with your back — thus you apply "back tension" — which transfers pressure to the third and fourth fingers and begins to rotate the release device. When you've rotated it far enough the string slips off the hook and you've made your shot.

For hunting, the index-finger trigger release aid is by far the most popular because it is the quickest and most natural to release. That's partly because you can "time" a shot with it and get off a shot quickly, something more difficult to do with the other styles. To a point that is good, but it can also be detrimental because it can lead to trigger punching and target panic. That's the value of the other styles. The little finger and thumb are less sensitive and responsive than the index finger, so the potential for target panic is reduced.

The back-tension release carries this concept one step further because you're essentially pulling with the large muscles of your back. Once you start exerting back pressure to rotate the release, you have little control over it. A majority of competitive archers use this style of release aid, because it assures the element of surprise, which is the basis for shooting accuracy. Few people hunt with this style, because you can't shoot quickly or time the shot. However, in reality that is the advantage. I personally have hunted with a back-tension release aid for many years and attribute many of my clean kills on game to the control demanded by this release aid.

**Fingers Release:** For shooting with fingers, the options are the finger glove and finger tab. Some traditional archers still shoot with three-stall finger gloves. I started shooting with this style many years ago myself. The problem is that your fingers are all individual, which makes getting a clean release somewhat difficult.

Many fingers shooters prefer a finger tab. Some tabs are padded, which reduces stress on the fingers, and the finger tab tends to spread the pressure across the three shooting fingers for a cleaner release. Some tabs also have a spacer between the index finger and middle finger to prevent pinching the nock of the arrow, a common problem for fingers shooters. Some archers pinch the nock so hard that they actually create a bend in the arrow. The "can't pinch" spacer reduces or eliminates this.

# Strings and Cables

String materials have evolved and improved greatly over the years. Prior to the late 1980s, essentially the only string material was Dacron. The one problem with Dacron is that it does stretch, which gives it a bit of inconsistency and makes it relatively slow. In 1989 Hoyt first introduced Fast Flight synthetic strings and cables into its bow line. The theme was "No More Tears," because the synthetic cables replaced traditional steel cables and teardrop attachments, which were always considered weak points in the cable system. Thus, the synthetic cables appeared to be the solution to a major flaw in cables. However, Fast Flight tends to creep over time. Thus, the string/cable systems continued to elongate over time, and the tune of the bow was constantly changing — as well as peep rotation in the string. In response to my grumbling about this, my wife commented, "No more tears? It looks like more tears to me."

The problem stemmed not just from lengthening of the material but slippage under the end servings. With experience Hoyt and other companies improved construction techniques to eliminate this problem. Along with this, the big string material makers, Brownell and BCY, developed another material called Vectran. The benefit of Vectran is that it is more stable than Fast Flight, eliminating stretching and creeping. The drawback is that Vectran

*The Carter index-finger-trigger release aid at top left has a sear that snaps over the string and cocks the trigger. The two T.R.U. Short-N-Sweet models below it simply hook onto the string. These release aids are identical except for trigger configuration. All of these release aids have wrist straps, and all can be easily adjusted in length.*

frays much more readily, so under tough hunting conditions the Vectran strings do not hold up nearly as well.

To address the stretching and fraying issues, the companies have combined Fast Flight and Vectran and another material called Dyneema to form blended materials such as S-4 and Ultra Cam from Brownell, and 450 Plus and 452X from BCY Fibers. These combinations give you the best of both worlds — durability and stability all in one string. Many of today's new bows come equipped with these blended strings, and overall these are probably the best choice. These strings should be waxed regularly to minimize fraying, but a good combination string should last two or three seasons if you maintain it well.

The nocking point is a critical part of any bowstring. The arrow must always fit on the string in exactly the same spot, so a solid nock locator is an essential part of any string. In the past most hunters used clamp-on nock locators. These are metal rings lined with soft plastic. You slide the opened ring onto the center serving and then, using special pliers, clamp the ring into place. For fingers shooting, a single nock locator is adequate. For shooting with a release aid, it's best to place a second nock locator directly above the first to prevent slippage, because the upward pressure exerted by the release aid will push a single locator up the serving. You can also wrap dental floss or serving thread above a single nock locator to hold it in place.

To cushion the nock of the arrow from the release aid, many hunters place an "eliminator button," a small rubber donut, just under the arrow so that the release aid pushes against the cushioning rubber, not against the arrow nock.

In recent years many release aid shooters have got away from the metal nockset in favor of a string loop. This is a short piece of cord tied into the string. The nock of the arrow fits inside of the loop, and the release aid is attached to the string loop rather than directly to the bowstring. The advantages are numerous: 1) The loop eliminates all release-aid wear on the bowstring; 2) it places the release aid directly behind the arrow, which eliminates the upward pressure against the nock; 3) it eliminates any torquing of the bowstring for cleaner arrow flight. Probably one of the biggest steps you can take toward getting clean arrow flight, especially with fixed-blade broadheads, is to install and shoot with a string loop.

Many hunters tie-in string loops with a length of cord about 4½ to 5 inches long. This works well, but it can be dangerous because, if not tied securely, one of the knots could slip out as you're drawing your bow — and guess where your knuckles will end up. You could easily lose some teeth or an eye. A safer loop is the ATI Super Loop, a one-piece loop that actually slips over the string to eliminate the potential for slippage. The all-metal QAD Ultra-Noc is a safe, simple alternative that clamps onto the string with screws.

## Quivers

Many years ago I was roaming the desert of eastern Oregon when I heard a terrible rattling sound in the distance. As it came closer I saw the source: a man with a bow in his hand had fash-

*Most bowhunters these days equip their bowstrings with string loops of one kind or another. At the top, the ATI Super Loop, a one-piece loop that slides over the string, is safe because it cannot slip or come untied. The metal Ultra-Noc is a safe, simple alternative that clamps onto the string with screws.*

*The back quiver with a shoulder strap is good for holding arrows on the practice range, but it's not a great choice for hunting.*

ioned a back quiver out of a cardboard box about 6 inches square. He had tied a rope to each end of the box and slung the whole rig over his shoulder. Instant back quiver! With a couple of dozen arrows stacked in there, he was a hunting machine, flying out across the sage — and rattling so loudly any deer within a mile or more would hear him coming. A quiver is a device to carry arrows in the field, so, okay, that guy had a quiver. But it might not have been the perfect choice.

Quivers can be broken into roughly three categories: back, hip, and bow. Let's examine the pros and cons of each.

**Back Quivers:** Some traditionalists still favor over-the-shoulder back quivers, and while this is a good way to carry a lot of arrows, these quivers do have their drawbacks. Noise is one. While many premium back quivers are made of soft leather, which collapses around the arrows to muffle the rattling to some degree, the fletching can still rub together to make some noise. In an open back quiver the broadheads can rub together, dulling them over time. When you bend over, the arrows can fall out of an open back quiver. And, finally, the arrows protruding above your shoulder can catch in the brush. Ultimately, tradition is the only real justification for hunting with an over-the-shoulder back quiver.

A popular alternative is the backpack-style back quiver. The best known of these is the Catquiver made by Rancho Safari. This quiver comes in numerous styles from a simple quiver with a couple of pouches at the top to a roomy backpack with a built-in quiver. The Catquiver holds arrows securely and quietly and protects both fletching and broadheads. It's probably the most popular hunting back quiver today.

**Hip Quivers:** Hip quivers were, at one time, relegated mostly to the practice range and tournament line, but in the 1990s they gained popularity among bowhunters, probably because of the influence of Chuck Adams. Adams successfully marketed his own leather hip quiver, and other manufacturers jumped on the bandwagon. Now many bowhunters use hip quivers.

*When I shot this caribou in Alaska, I was using a Carter Revenger back-tension release aid.*

A good hip quiver holds arrows securely and silently in ready position for quick access. The main argument against hip quivers is that the nock ends of the arrows stick out behind you and potentially can snag in brush to distract you or make noise. For a tree stand hunter who does not like to shoot with a quiver on his bow, the hip quiver is a good choice because he can either leave it on his belt or remove it and hang it beside his stand.

***Bow Quiver:*** The year 1946 was a turning point for quivers, because that's the year Fred Bear introduced a revolutionary product — the bow quiver. In his book *Fred Bear,* Charles Kroll writes, "The bow quiver patent, entered in 1946, was one of the very few to go through the patent office with absolutely no references cited."

The bow quiver became almost universal as hunters quickly recognized the convenience and reliability of a good bow quiver. What are the strong points of bow quivers? Convenience ranks at the top. With a bow quiver, your bow and arrows become one unit that is easy to maneuver through the brush, and the arrows are held in position for quick access. A good quiver holds the arrows securely for safety and silence.

In buying a bow quiver, insist on a solid hood with deep foam that completely hides the broadheads to prevent cutting yourself. The arrow grippers should be snug enough to hold the shafts tightly. Most companies make both carbon and aluminum grippers, so buy the model that holds your shafts most securely. Also, look for a quiver with the broadhead hood and shaft grippers 20 inches or more apart so that long ends of the arrows are not left hanging out to rattle together with each shot.

The number of arrows your quiver holds is a matter of personal preference. Like most bowhunters, I used to use a standard eight-arrow quiver. But I rarely shot more than one or two arrows, and frankly I didn't like the bulk and weight of an eight-arrow quiver. So I switched to a four-arrow model, which I have used for many years. I carry three broadhead-tipped arrows and a blunt-tipped practice arrow. I have never — knock on wood — needed more arrows than that in a day of hunting.

Some hunters like the convenience of quivers that can quickly be detached from their bows, especially for tree stand hunting. For convenience, they generally carry the quiver full of arrows to their stands and then remove the quiver from the bow and hang it in the tree because they prefer to shoot without the quiver attatched to the bow. These hunters usually practice without quivers on their bows, so they want to hunt the same way. That makes some sense, because a bow might shoot slightly differently with and without the quiver. However, I prefer just to practice with the quiver on my bow, and I've never felt it hampered accuracy, especially at close, tree stand distances.

The one situation in which a bow quiver can become a liability is in stiff wind. The quiver and its load of arrows create a fairly major wind resistance, which can cause excessive bow movement. Overall, however, I see the bow quiver as an excellent bowhunting accessory. I personally can't imagine hunting without a quiver mounted on my bow.

## Additional Items

**Wrist Sling:** This might seem like an insignificant item, one strictly of personal preference, but in terms of shooting accuracy, the wrist sling might be the most valuable item you can attach to your bow. That's because to shoot accurately you must keep a loose, open bow hand, and that's possible only with a wrist sling. Without the sling, you will be forced to grip or grab your bow to keep it from falling to the ground.

Most wrist slings screw into the stabilizer bushing. My favorite wrist sling is made of braided leather, because this sling retains its shape so you can easily slide your hand in and out. Thus, in a hunting situation, you can quickly slide your hand into the sling, ready to shoot instantly. (For more on wrist slings, see Chapter 4.)

**Silencing Devices:** In recent years, bow silencing has become an industry unto itself. Even the best bows are no more than about 80 percent efficient. That means that 80 percent of the energy stored in a bow is transferred to the arrow, which is exceptional for a mechanical device. But it still leaves 20 percent of the bow's energy to go somewhere else, and the "somewhere else" is the bow itself. Most of the excess energy not transferred to the arrow ripples through the bow and manifests itself in the form of vibration and noise.

Bow design, draw weight, quality of construction, and other variables could affect noise levels. In the past, the most rudimentary silencing devices were string silencers placed in the string to dampen string vibration, and, on stickbows, these were about all that were needed. Silencers placed in the string 6 to 8 inches from each limb tip would dramatically reduce the *twang!* so noticeable with each shot.

Compound bows, however, store more energy and thus create more excess energy, and they have more mechanical parts to rattle and vibrate. So silencing a compound bow can be a little more detailed. String silencers are a good starting point on all bows. These can take many forms — yarn puffs, strips of PolarFleece, rubber bands, rubber "cat whiskers." I prefer silencers made of rubber, particularly the cat whiskers, because they work well and do not absorb moisture and become damp and moldy. Sims String Leeches are excellent new string silencers.

To install silencers, separate the strands of the bowstring roughly in half, 6 inches or so from the limb tip. If you have a bow press, relax the bow slightly and slip the silencing material

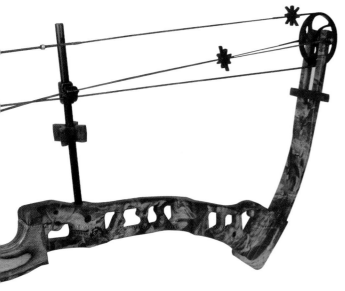

For silence, the BowTech Patriot comes equipped with string and cable silencers, a rubber cable-guard stop, and VibraBlocks limb vibration dampeners.

between the strands. If you don't have a press, work a dull screwdriver that won't fray the string between the strands to separate the strands far enough to slip the silencer through, and tie the silencer in place. Install a silencer on each end of the string.

A lot of compound bow noise can come strictly from loose screws and parts. Periodically go through your entire bow with an Allen-wrench set and tighten all screws. A drop of Loc-Tite or rubber cement on the threads will keep screws from loosening. Or you can place a drop of epoxy on the head of the screw and the mounting surface.

Any number of other silencing devices are available. Sims Limb Savers, rubbery buttons placed near the end of each bow limb, significantly reduce vibration and noise in some bows. And other Sims devices, such as cable-guard dampeners, can help reduce noise as well. A stabilizer also helps to reduce noise by absorbing and dampening vibration.

This all refers primarily to noise created by the shot, but other noises can ruin hunting opportunities. If you tap an arrow against the bow shelf or sight window at just the wrong time, you could chase off the buck of a lifetime. To prevent that, cover the shelf and sight window with soft material. Neet and other companies make camouflaged, self-adhesive moleskin ideal for this purpose.

Even more critical is silencing your arrow rest so you can come to full draw without any hissing or squeaking as your arrow slides across the rest. The slightest drawing sound will cost you shots at close-range deer and bears on calm, quiet days, so never cut corners in silencing your arrow rest. Moleskin works well for silencing some arrow rests, although it wears down and must be replaced occasionally. A better material on rests with flat support blades is Bears Hair, sold by Bear Archery. It's made as rug rest for stickbows, but the adhesive-backed carpeting makes excellent silencing material for all rests. For prong-style rests, shrink tube is probably the best silencing material. Whatever material you choose, you want to be able to draw your arrow absolutely silently.

**Stabilizers:** Stabilizers come in many forms and have many functions. Some stabilizers are simple steel or aluminum rods with weights on the end, some incorporate rubber bushings, others have interchangeable weights, and some work on a hydraulic principle.

Stabilizers have several functions. You've probably seen tournament archers, both Olympic style (recurve) and compound shooters with long stabilizers protruding out the front and both sides of their bows. These stabilizers add weight, and thus stability; they prevent torque, or twisting; and they balance the bows. In tournaments where fractions of an inch in arrow placement mean the difference between winning and losing, such stabilizers play a major role.

A stabilizer performs similar functions on a hunting bow, although the need for perfection is not as great. If your average shot distance is 20 yards or less from a tree stand, the addition of a stabilizer should not be needed for accuracy.

A stabilizer can significantly improve the balance of some hunting bows. When you release the string, a bow should stand up in your hand or tip slowly forward. That way the arrow rest is tilting forward out of the way of the arrow. Most bows with straight or reflexed handles do tip forward, and on those, in my opinion, you really do not need a stabilizer for balance. However, if you shoot a bow with a deflexed riser, the top limb of the bow will tip back toward you after the shot, and a stabilizer can greatly improve balance by tipping the bow forward. You have to experiment to see how long and heavy of a stabilizer you need to balance your bow.

The other major value of a stabilizer on a hunting bow is noise and vibration reduction. As pointed out above, when you shoot a bow, 20 percent or more of the energy ripples through the bow to create noise, vibration, and hand shock. The higher performance the bow — i.e., faster — the greater these side effects. A good stabilizer will absorb much of the vibration, thus making the bow more comfortable to shoot and somewhat quieter.

Among hunters, the most popular stabilizers are short "hunting" stabilizers. The Saunders Boostizer and Tamer V-4 stabilizers come in three lengths and offer many combinations of "node harmonic tuning combinations." Doinker stabilizers use rubber weights to "isolate" vibration from the bow. If your bow "kicks" or produces excessive noise, then the addition of a short hunting stabilizer may make the bow somewhat more pleasant to shoot. Golden Key-Futura specializes in hydraulic stabilizers that dampen sound and give the bow a "soft" feel.

Some hunters think a stabilizer is needed for weight. While a heavy bow can be more stable than a lighter bow simply because it better resists outside forces like hand torque and wind, I think most bows are plenty heavy without the stabilizer. Many compound bows equipped with arrow rest, sights, and bow quiver, weigh more than 6 pounds, and I doubt they'll shoot significantly better just because you increase the weight to 7 or 8 pounds with a stabilizer. Besides, the trend these days is toward lighter-weight hunting bows. Many companies tout their bows that weigh as little as 3 pounds — or less. It seems a little ironic to me when a guy buys a 3-pound bow and sticks a 3-pound stabilizer on it. Why not just buy a heavier bow?

Some stabilizers reduce noise without adding much weight. In this sense, they aren't really so much stabilizers as silencers. The Golden Key-Futura Tranquilizer is a good example. It weighs mere ounces, but using Sims noise-dampening technology, it helps to quiet a bow.

In most situations, I personally do not use a stabilizer on my hunting bows, particularly in hunting the backcountry where I might be hiking several miles a day. An added pound or two in the hand can multiply fatigue quickly. And if a bow is so rough and noisy that it demands a stabilizer, my preference would be to buy a milder-shooting bow.

One situation in which I have found a stabilizer to be useful is in stalking. I have a 10-inch Vibracheck with a rubber tip on it. When crawling through the sagebrush after a mule deer or antelope, holding my bow in my right hand, this stabilizer makes an excellent "peg leg" to help in stalking.

*The Doinker is a popular hunting stabilizer. This short model with a rubber insert helps to balance and silence a bow, yet it does not get in the way.*

*For realistic hunting practice, invest in a good 3-D target. In hunting camp, Merrill Jones practices on a McKenzie deer to tune up for the hunt. On foam 3-D targets like this, you can practice with both field points and broadheads. This model has a replaceable core.*

## Practice Targets

For general practice with field points, you would have a hard time beating a good "bean bag" target like the Morrell Eternity Target. Essentially this model consists of a burlap or plastic cover stuffed with cotton batting or similar material. Bean bags will stop the fastest arrows, yet you easily can pull your arrows with two fingers. If the target gets a little "shot out," you can pound it to redistribute the stuffing. You can set a bean bag target outside in your yard or hang it in your shop or basement for a safe backstop. Indian Cord grass targets from Saunders Archery also make good general practice butts. If taken care of, these targets will last for years. Arrows don't pull as easily as they do from bean bag targets. You might want to use a wrap-around arrow puller to extract your arrows from a cord grass target.

Choosing a good target butt for broadheads is not so simple. Some of the most popular are made of laminated foam of varying densities. When a broadhead passes through the target, the foam layers tend to re-seal the channels cut by broadheads, and the targets thus hold up pretty well to the abuse of broadheads. For general broadhead tuning and practice, laminated foam is about as good as you will find. The arrows come out fairly easily, and the targets hold up well, although, like any broadhead targets, they will eventually be cut to pieces.

These days 3-D targets are the big rage. Companies like McKenzie and Delta make whole herds of realistic 3-D animal targets. If you're going on a bear or antelope hunt — animals with which you are not familiar — it is wise to shoot targets that simulate those you'll be hunting.

These targets are good for both field points and broadheads. You may need an arrow puller to pull your arrows from some 3-D targets. To make extraction a little easier, you can wipe your arrows with a silicone agent that makes the surface slicker.

## Rangefinders

Years ago hunters practiced long and hard to develop range-estimating skills, and such practice can still be valuable. But modern rangefinders have eliminated much of the need for intuitive rangefinding.

The Ranging Company first popularized hand-held rangefinders with its optical rangefinders. On these you looked into a viewfinder, which showed two images of the target, and turned a dial until the images came together to form one image. You then read the distance off the dial. These optical rangefinders served bowhunters well for many years.

Then along came the laser rangefinder, and today most bowhunters shooting with sights rely heavily on laser rangefinders. These vary in price and capability, but a bowhunter hardly needs a rangefinder capable of one-yard accuracy at 1,000 yards. A lightweight, simple rangefinder like the Bushnell Yardage Pro Scout, which weighs a mere 6.8 ounces and can be operated with one hand, is an excellent choice for bowhunting. It has an eyepiece with 6X magnification and a maximum accuracy range of about 300 yards.

In hunting open-country animals like antelope and mule deer, you may be able to take a reading directly on the animal, and that is ideal. However, in many cases you will not have time to do this. And often it can frustrate you to no end because of obstructions. If even the slightest twig or blade of grass lies between you and your target, your rangefinder will read off that obstruction, not your target.

That's why in many cases, and particularly in stand hunting, you're better off to use your rangefinder to gauge the distance to trees, bushes, and rocks around your stand well before any animals show up. Then you will instantly know the distance when an animal approaches one of your pre-ranged landmarks.

## Bow Cases

To protect your bow when you travel, buy a good bow case. This is not a good place to scrimp, because cheap bow cases not only will not protect your bow well, but they will not last through many trips. If you travel a lot, you're far better off buying one good case than three or four cheap ones.

One of the most popular among serious traveling bowhunters is the SKB Double Bow Case. Like most bow cases, it contains thick foam padding to protect your bow and arrows. Most experienced travelers remove all the foam padding and then pack all their hunting clothes around their bows and other gear. That way the bow case doubles as a duffel bag, and the clothing offers as good as or better protection than the foam does. You can do the same with any hard-side case made of molded plastic or aluminum.

An alternative is to use a soft-side case in a similar way. For years I have traveled with my Mathews bow case made of Cordura nylon. I simply fill the soft case with my fleece clothing, longjohns, socks, and T-shirts and then nestle my bow among all these clothes. With this system I have flown to Alaska, Canada, and all over the Lower 48 and have never had any problems with my bows. As added security, I wrap a nylon compression strap around the case and snug it down as tight as possible, just in case the zipper should ever fail.

Commercial arrow tubes are available, but many are bigger than necessary. I have made my own arrow tubes out of 4-inch PVC pipe. I then pack this inside my soft bow case or in my duffel bag. This system has never failed me.

*The SKB Bow Case is one of the most rugged bow cases made. Some hunters remove the foam padding and pack clothing around their bows.*

*Chapter 3*

# Arrows

It would be easy to draw an analogy between arrows for a bow and ammo for a rifle, and to some degree that is valid. However, the analogy breaks down, because with rifle ammo you would select a bullet for a particular animal. For example, if you shoot a .30-06, you might choose a 130-grain bullet for deer and a 180-grain bullet for elk. You're matching the bullet to the animal.

In archery, most people would not match their "ammo" to the animal, but rather to the bow. In that sense, choosing arrows is more like choosing line for a fly rod. In order to get the rod to cast right, you do not match the line to the fish but to the rod. And so it is with a bow.

## Shaft Materials

Prior to 1939, wood was essentially the only arrow shaft choice. Then, in 1939, Doug Easton introduced his revolutionary new aluminum shafts, and the arrow market changed forever. Since that time aluminum has dominated the arrow market, and for

*One of my staple hunting shafts has been the Easton A/C/C 3-49. With a total weight of 440 grains, these arrows have proven efficient on all big game animals. I took this kudu in South Africa.*

*In terms of mass weight and spine, aluminum gives you a wide range of options. Shown here, front to back, are Easton XX75 shafts in size 1816, 2020, 2013, 2016, and 2413. The variations in diameter and wall thickness dictate spine and weight.*

good reason. Aluminum arrows are precision made, durable, handsome with their many fine camo finishes, and reasonably priced. Perhaps best of all, aluminum arrows come in a multitude of sizes and grades to match every situation. In its 2004 catalog, Easton lists 27 sizes of aluminum bowhunting shafts from which you can pick the shafts that best match your bow.

Many compound shooters still prefer large-diameter aluminum arrows because these shafts assure plenty of fletching clearance through the arrow rest. While this has changed to some degree with the introduction of "fat" carbon shafts, aluminum arrows remain easy to tune and shoot accurately. Many traditional archers favor aluminum arrows, partly because of the heavy mass weight. With heavyweights like the Easton XX75 2020, which weighs 13.49 grains per inch, and XX75 2219 (13.77 grains per inch), traditionalists get maximum arrow stability and kinetic energy from their stickbows. And shafts in the XX75 Legacy series boast a wood-grain finish that fits right in with the traditional concept.

The bad news about aluminum arrows is that they bend. The good news is that you can straighten them. I have straightened aluminum practice arrows many times and they last for years. However, I use only new, factory-straight shafts for hunting. If you shoot aluminums, a quality arrow straightener is worth the price. You can also straighten broadheads with it. Easton sells aluminum arrows at several price points, depending on the alloy used, construction method, straightness and weight tolerances, nock-attachment system, and camo pattern. Thus, you should match your arrow selection to your wallet.

Up through the 1980s, aluminum arrows probably captured more than 90 percent of the total arrow market. Wood arrows held on with traditionalists, and a few fiberglass and carbon arrows came and went. But none of these had the consistency and accuracy of aluminum. So aluminum remained king.

In the 1990s carbon technology took off, and now carbon arrows are pushing aluminum for supremacy. The primary reason is light weight in relation to spine. That is, carbon arrows can be made both stiff and light at the same time, a combination that appeals to anyone seeking maximum arrow speed.

Early carbon arrows were made by a "pultrusion" process, where the fibers were pulled over a mandrel to form them into a shaft. Thus, the carbon fibers ran parallel for the length of the shaft. Many early pultruded shafts were far from straight, which did not elicit confidence among precision-minded bowhunters. Also, the shafts were very small in diameter — many critics disdainfully called them "soda straws" — which posed two problems: 1) The support arms on an arrow rest had to be so close together to hold a shaft that getting complete fletching clearance was nearly impossible; 2) Nocks and broadhead adaptors would not fit inside the tiny shafts, so components were mounted with "outserts," which slipped over the outside of the shafts. Outserts created a clubby appearance and contact problems with the arrow rest. To seal the stigma, early carbon shafts came in only one color — black.

In the mid-'90s, "wrapped" carbon technology changed all of this. Wrapped shafts were large enough in diameter to accept internal components and assure complete fletching clearance. And these newer shafts were precision made, rivaling aluminum in terms of straightness and weight tolerances. Carbon shafts are now available in camo and wood-grain patterns.

They're also available in many diameters, spine values, and mass weights. Depending on brand, you can get carbon shafts weighing anywhere from 5.5 grains per inch for maximum speed up to 11 grains per inch for maximum kinetic energy. Many companies — Gold Tip, Game Tracker, Beman, Easton, Carbon Tech, Carbon Impact, among others — now produce top-quality carbon shafts.

To my knowledge, no scientific studies prove that carbon arrows penetrate better than aluminum and wood arrows, but many hunters — their judgments are based strictly on experience — believe they do. Relatively small diameter and the stiff nature of carbon could contribute to good penetration. Many traditionalists avidly shoot carbon arrows. Some particularly like the original pultruded arrows like Beman Carbon Hunters, because on non-center-shot bows, these small-diameter arrows sit closer to center than fatter shafts do.

For bowhunters who want small-diameter arrows without the bulky outserts, Easton has developed its Axis arrows. These shafts are scarcely bigger than pultruded shafts, but they have totally internal components. Most carbon arrow makers sort their arrows according to straightness. Those with the greatest variables are sold as economy models, while those with the tightest tolerances bring a premium price.

Aluminum/carbon shafts, which have an aluminum core overlaid with several wraps of carbon, combine the best of both worlds. With the aluminum core, these shafts can be factory-straightened to precise tolerances. And with the carbon exterior, the shafts have the durability and penetrating qualities of other carbon arrows. The Easton A/C/C 3-49, weighing 8.83 grains per inch, has been my staple hunting arrow for years. My finished arrows, with 125-grain broadheads and plastic vanes installed weigh 440 grains, and these arrows, shot from a 55-pound compound, have performed flawlessly on deer, elk, moose, caribou, and African game.

The newer Easton A/C Kinetic, which comes standard with a classy camo finish, offers the same rugged precision as the A/C/C but in slightly heavier weights (up to 11.64 grains per inch) for maximum penetration on oversized animals. The Beman Carbonmetal Matrix is a similar A/C shaft built for accuracy and penetration. A/C arrows do not come in different quality

*For bows that are not cut to center, arrow spine must be precise, because the arrows must flex around the handle of the bow and then return to the shooter's line of sight to the target.*

and price grades. They're all precision made, expensive, and they're worth the price.

Wood arrows made of cedar, ash, maple, fir, and other woods are still available, and many serious traditionalists would think of shooting nothing else. Custom wood arrows are works of art, and if they're carefully sorted according to spine and mass weight they shoot as well as any other arrows. That's the caveat — if they're carefully sorted. Wood varies greatly in density and grain, so not all wood shafts are created equal. Producing a matched set requires time and knowledge, and, as a result, perfectly matched custom wood arrows are expensive.

The other drawback to wood is its fragility. In wet weather, wood arrows will warp, no matter how good the finish, and if stored in a bent position, they will take a set. Also, a wood arrow could crack after slapping into a target or animal. Check wood arrows after each shot, or you could get an armful of splinters on the next use. The bottom line is, if tradition is your game, wood arrows are for you. Otherwise, stick with aluminum or carbon.

If you're just getting into bowhunting, I would recommend you start with Easton Gamegetter aluminum or lower-end wrapped carbon shafts. You won't get too upset over breaking or losing a few of these economy shafts. As you gain experience and confidence, you'll want to shoot the best. At that point, treat yourself to some Easton XX78 or XX75 aluminum shafts, high-end carbon shafts, or Easton or Beman A/C shafts.

# Spine Weight

Spine relates to stiffness, and this is the first variable to consider in choosing arrows for your particular bow. When you shoot a bow, the arrow does not slide straight off the rest. Rather, the instant you release the bowstring, the arrow bends and oscillates radically. A number of slow-motion videos demonstrate this point. Watch one of these and you will see that an arrow released with fingers oscillates violently in a horizontal plane, much like a salmon swimming against the current. That's because, as the string slips off your fingers, it is pushed to the left (for a right-handed shooter). As the string moves left, the arrow reacts by bending to the right. It then bends left, then right, "swimming" forward toward the target. The fact is, a properly spined arrow, released with fingers, remains in contact with the arrow rest no more than about 6 inches. It then flexes out away from the rest and is free flying well before it clears the bow.

In contrast, an arrow released with a release aid generally oscillates up and down, much like a porpoise swimming through the water. The degree of oscillation depends on the stiffness of the arrow, timing of the bow's cam (or cams), nock placement, and other variables. It can range from violent whipping to virtually no oscillation. Generally, a release-aid-shot arrow remains in contact with the arrow rest for its full length.

To get arrows to fly well, they must be spined correctly for your bow. In general, the heavier the draw weight, the stiffer the arrows must be. You can consult manufacturers' charts to find which shaft they recommend for any given draw weight and style of bow.

For stickbows, arrow spine is far more critical than for most compounds. That's particularly true for bows that do not have a sight window cut to center. With such bows, arrow spine value must be close to perfect so that the arrows bend around the handle of the bow and return to your line of sight to hit the target. If the spine is too weak, arrows will hit right of the target, if too stiff, left of the target. This is particularly critical if you're shooting without sights, because the arrows must strike precisely where you're looking.

Incidentally, this is where the term "paradox" comes from. With bows not cut to center, which describes most longbows and a lot of recurves, the arrow, string, and bow are not in line with the target when you aim. If you line up the bowstring with the center of a longbow, and then line these up with the target, you'll see that a nocked arrow actually points far left of the target (for a right-handed shooter). Yet, when you release the string that arrow comes back into line with the bull's-eye. That is a paradox — a seeming contradiction. Some people use the word paradox loosely to refer to the bending of the arrow, but that is not correct.

With modern compound bows and modern shooting methods, spine is not, in my opinion, nearly as critical. A release aid, string loop, and flexible arrow rest greatly reduce oscillation and its effects on arrow flight. Besides, if spine is off a little and your arrows group slightly off target, you can simply move your bowsight to bring the arrows into the bull's-eye, a luxury you don't have shooting barebow. Thus, with modern tackle you have more leeway in relation to spine. Nonetheless, the more closely you match arrows to your bow, the easier your tackle will tune and the more accurately you will shoot.

A number of variables affect spine value of arrows. The most basic of these is shaft construction. In general, the larger the diameter of the shafts, the stiffer. Wall thickness also affects spine value, and the thicker the walls of the shaft, the stiffer. Easton aluminum shafts are defined by a four-digit number like 2213. The first two numbers define diameter in 64ths of an inch. Thus, a 2213 is $\frac{22}{64}$ inch in diameter. The second two numbers relate to wall thickness in thousandths of an inch. Thus, the wall of a 2213 is .013 inch thick.

The same principle applies to carbon arrows although each manufacturer has its own system for rating spine value. Spine value of wood shafts is dictated largely by the diameter and density of the wood's grain.

Other factors also control spine. Shaft length is one. The longer a shaft of a given construction, the more flexible it is. Thus, a 30-inch 2213 aluminum shaft has a weaker spine value than a 25-inch 2213. Point weight also affects spine. On any given shaft, the heavier the point, the weaker the spine of the arrow. Thus, if you go from a 100-grain broadhead to a 125-grain broadhead, you weaken the spine of the arrow. To put that another way, the arrow will flex more with the heavier head installed. If you change head weight, you normally have to change shaft size.

## Arrow Weight

Arrow weight refers to the physical, or mass, weight of the arrow. Generally, arrows are weighed in grains (437.5 grains equal 1 ounce). While physical weight and spine value of arrows are related, they are, to some degree, independent of each other. For example, if you look at the Easton spine chart you will see that for a bow with soft cams, 60-pound draw weight, and 30-inch draw length, you can choose from eight hunting shafts with similar spine values — but with mass weights varying from 215 grains to 323 grains (shaft weight only).

What weight shafts should you shoot? This has always been subject to debate. Arrow weight affects two major variables: arrow speed (thus, trajectory); and arrow energy (thus, penetration). Archers who want maximum speed and the flattest-possible trajectory advocate shooting lightweight arrows. Those who want to maximize penetration advocate shooting heavy arrows.

Both views have pros and cons. Indeed, ultralight arrows do shoot flatter, which can be an advantage at unknown distances. And greater speed reduces the chance that an animal will jump the string. However, increased speed comes with a price. At the shot, arrows absorb part of a bow's energy, and the heavier the arrow the more of that energy the arrow absorbs. Because excess energy vibrating through a bow causes both noise and potential damage to the bow, heavier arrows tend to shoot quieter and safer.

Here is a physical truth: The heavier an arrow, the greater percentage of a bow's energy it will absorb. To put that into precise figures, assume a 60-pound bow shoots a 400-grain arrow at 260 fps. At that level, the arrow would initially produce 60 foot-pounds (fp) of K.E. Now let's increase the arrow weight to 600 grains. That would drop the arrow speed to roughly 220 fps, but it would increase the K.E. to about 64.5 fp. That is an immutable truth — all else remaining equal, an increase in arrow weight reduces arrow speed but increases K.E.

In addition, speed in itself can have shortcomings. The faster an arrow, the more critical it is to shoot. You may find you have accuracy problems shooting arrows at 300 fps that you did not have at 250 fps. That's especially true if you shoot large, fixed-blade broadheads.

Also, think about this: Most whitetail deer are killed at distances of 20 yards and closer where super-flat trajectory is hardly required. In western hunting, particularly when stalking, distances can be farther and flat trajectory gives a decided advantage. However, modern rangefinders eliminate the guesswork in range estimation, so even in western hunting, ultra-flat trajectory is not as critical as it once was.

Many archers conclude that you should always shoot the heaviest arrows possible from any given bow. I don't agree with that. In the above example, you gain only 7.5 percent in K.E. by increasing arrow weight 200 grains, but you lose 40 fps in speed. Considering that the 400-grain arrow produces 60 fp of K.E. — more than enough power for any game in North America — you

## Arrow Shot with Fingers
*(Overhead view)*

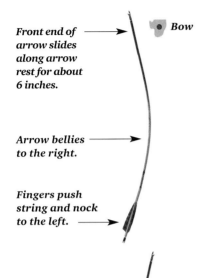

Front end of arrow slides along arrow rest for about 6 inches. → **Bow**

Arrow bellies to the right. →

Fingers push string and nock to the left. →

Arrow flexes the opposite way and bellies to the left — it has now swung out away from the bow handle and arrow rest. → **Bow**

Arrow bellies back to the right as it travels past bow handle. →

Fletching swings out and around arrow rest. → **Bow**

## Arrow Shot with Release Aid
*(Side view)*

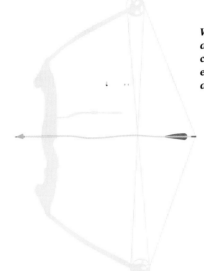

**When shot with a release aid, an arrow flexes vertically. It stays in contact with the arrow rest its entire length (unless a fall-away arrow rest is used).**

## AMO Recommended Minimum Arrow Weights *(Grains)*

**Using the Minimum Recommended Arrow Weight Chart**

- Select the column that describes the type of bow you shoot
- Move down the column to locate your Actual Peak Bow Weight
- Move horizontally across that row to your "AMO Draw Length" column
- The box at that location contains the minimum total arrow weight recommended for your equipment.

1. Arrow weight includes all arrow componets — shaft, insert, point, fletching and nock.
2. Based on: 360-Grain Arrow • 30" Draw Length • 60# Peak Weight
   • Speed Cam SE = Stored Energy • ESE = Energy Storage Efficiency
   • BH = Brace Height • PDF = Peak Draw Force

| ACTUAL PEAK BOW WEIGHT IN LBS. | | | | 25" | 26" | 27" | 28" | 29" | 30" | 31" | 32" | 33" |
|---|---|---|---|---|---|---|---|---|---|---|---|---|
| RECOVERY<br>SE=.950<br>PDF<br>ESE=62<br>BH=9.5 | ROUND WHEEL<br>SE=1.04<br>PDF<br>ESE=65.6<br>BH=9.0 | ENERGY WHEEL<br>SE=1.20<br>PDF<br>ESE=71.3<br>BH=8.0 | SPEED CAM<br>SE=1.3+<br>PDF<br>ESE=75.1<br>BH=7.0 | | | | | | | | | |
| 33 | 32 | 29 | 27 | 150 | 150 | 150 | 150 | 150 | 150 | 150 | 150 | 150 |
| 34-41 | 33-38 | 30-35 | 28-32 | 150 | 150 | 150 | 150 | 150 | 150 | 150 | 151 | 165 |
| 42-46 | 39-43 | 36-39 | 33-36 | 150 | 150 | 150 | 150 | 150 | 163 | 179 | 195 | 211 |
| 47-52 | 44-49 | 40-44 | 37-41 | 150 | 150 | 150 | 167 | 185 | 203 | 222 | 240 | 258 |
| 53-58 | 50-54 | 45-49 | 42-46 | 150 | 163 | 183 | 203 | 224 | 244 | 264 | 285 | 305 |
| 59-63 | 55-60 | 50-54 | 47-50 | 172 | 195 | 217 | 240 | 262 | 284 | 307 | 329 | 352 |
| 64-69 | 61-64 | 55-59 | 51-55 | 202 | 227 | 251 | 276 | 300 | 325 | 350 | 374 | 399 |
| 70-75 | 65-71 | 60-64 | 56-60 | 232 | 259 | 286 | 312 | 339 | 365 | 392 | 419 | 445 |
| 76-81 | 72-76 | 65-70 | 61-65 | 262 | 291 | 320 | 348 | 377 | 406 | 435 | 463 | 492 |
| 82-86 | 77-81 | 71-74 | 66-69 | 292 | 323 | 354 | 385 | 416 | 446 | 477 | 508 | 539 |
| 87-92 | 82-87 | 75-79 | 70-74 | 322 | 355 | 388 | 421 | 454 | 487 | 520 | 553 | 586 |
| 93-99 | 88-94 | 80-85 | 75-80 | 352 | 387 | 422 | 457 | 492 | 532 | 581 | 629 | 676 |

*For shooting whitetail deer at 20 yards, you don't need the extremes of arrow weight, either light or heavy. A compromise in arrow weight generally will be the best choice. A midweight arrow will perform well on deer, like this whitetail I shot in Texas.*

probably lose more than you gain. If you were shooting a lightweight bow that produced only 40 fp of K.E., a marginal level for larger game, you might be well advised to shoot the heaviest arrow possible to maximize energy. But in shooting a bow with 50 fp of K.E. or greater, you can lose a bit of energy to improve trajectory.

What is the bottom line for arrow weight? Somewhere in the middle is the best choice. There is little reason to go to the extremes of heavy or light. In the midrange of arrow weight you essentially gain the advantages of both extremes without any of the serious drawbacks.

In the days before compound bows, many bowhunters followed the standard of 9 grains of arrow weight per pound of draw weight. Thus, the recommended arrow weight for a 60-pound bow would be 540 grains. With modern tackle, that standard is pretty much obsolete. For hunting any animals from deer to moose, arrows weighing between 400 and 600 grains should more than do the job.

The Archery Trade Association has developed a chart of recommended minimum arrow weights. For a compound bow of 60-pound draw weight, and 30-inch draw length, the recommended weight is 6 grains of arrow weight per pound of draw weight. For bows lighter in draw weight or shorter in draw length, the grain weight can be decreased to less than 6 grains per pound of draw weight, and for heavier bows the grain weight would be increased to more than 6 grains per pound of draw weight. If you stay within the guidelines of the ATA chart, your bow will perform fine.

## Components

***Fletching:*** The two options here are feathers or plastic vanes, and both have their proponents. Feathers are lighter. Three 5-inch feathers weigh less than 10 grains, while three 5-inch vanes weigh 30 to 40 grains (depending on manufacturer). Thus, all else being equal, a feather-fletched shaft has a faster initial speed than does a vane-fletched shaft. However, because feathers have more drag (air resistance) they slow down faster. So at some distance, probably around 50 to 60 yards, a vane-fletched arrow will be traveling at the same speed as a feather-fletched arrow — all else being equal. (The feather-fletched arrow will still reach the target quicker, because it has a faster average speed, but the difference in elapsed time is negligible at most hunting distances.) Note also that vanes add more weight to the rear of the arrow. So you must use a heavier head/insert combination to maintain adequate weight-forward balance of the arrow with vanes.

Probably the major argument for feathers is their forgiving nature. Because they have more drag, they tend to stabilize arrows with fixed-blade broadheads better than vanes do. Also, because feathers are more flexible, they will slide smoothly across an arrow rest, whereas plastic vanes will deflect off the rest and cause wobbly arrow flight. For this reason, it's easier to get good arrow flight with feather-fletched arrows, and accuracy might be slightly better. However, if you use a quality shoot-through or fall-away rest that minimizes or eliminates fletching contact, you would be hard pressed to see any difference in arrow flight and accuracy between arrows fletched with feathers or vanes. Of course, if you shoot off the shelf with a stickbow, your arrows must be fletched with feathers. Vanes will deflect off the shelf and sight window. Feathers slide smoothly over the shelf.

The main argument in favor of vanes is durability. Good vanes hold up to a beating and are impervious to moisture. I've been shooting some vane-fletched arrows for more than 10 years. They've been shot through targets, rattled through brush, and gotten soaked with rain and they're as functional now as the day they were fletched. Feathers, in contrast, are relatively fragile. Once through a target will tear them up, and they will simply wear out over time. And in wet weather, they become matted. Treating them with waterproofing helps, but is not a perfect solution. Many feathers shooters cover their fletching with a plastic bag in wet weather.

Vanes also are quieter. Feathers accidentally brushed against a twig or your clothing can make a scraping sound that will spook close game. Plastic vanes in a similar situation are silent.

*These three 5-inch feathers weigh 9.8 grains. Because the feathers weigh about 30 grains less than three vanes, an arrow fletched with the feathers will have a faster initial arrow speed.*

Then come several other questions commonly asked about fletching: Should you shoot three fletch or four fletch? Four or five-inch fletching? Helical or straight fletching? Right or left twist?

Three-fletch has more space between the fletchings for better rest clearance, but four-fletch gives a little more surface area for more stable arrow flight, and four-fletch, being symmetrical, can be nocked either way. For large broadheads, 5-inch fletching will provide a little more stability. For smaller broadheads or open-on-impact broadheads, 4-inch fletching will provide adequate steerage, and some people prefer the smaller fletchings because they give a little better rest clearance and, because they're lighter than 5 inches, slightly more speed.

For large broadheads, helical fletching (twisted around the shaft) may help increase accuracy. If you're using a shoot-through rest, however, you may have trouble getting complete fletching clearance with a heavy helical. That's why many release-aid shooters fletch their arrows with straight fletching slightly offset. Most traditional archers shooting large broadheads prefer a strong helical in their feather fletching.

In the old days, there was a myth that right-handed shooters should twist or offset their fletching to the right, and lefties to the left. In reality, it makes no difference. Right-handers often shoot with left-helical fletching. The direction of twist matters only in relation to which wing feathers are used. Feathers from the right wings of birds must be twisted to the right, and those from left wings to the left. Plastic vanes can be twisted either way, because they have no grain. The main thing is to fletch all your arrows the same way.

This can sound pretty complicated, so let me tell you how I fletch my arrows as a guide to get you started: For compound bows with a release aid and shoot-through rest, I fletch my arrows with three, 5-inch vanes, glued on straight but offset 1 or 2 degrees to the right. I have had excellent results shooting fixed-blade broadheads with this fletching. I prefer vanes because they're quieter and more durable. For shooting traditional bows, I fletch my arrows with three 5-inch, right wing feathers glued on with a moderate helical twist to the right. With experience, you might want to try different fletching configurations.

*Nocks:* The nock may seem like a small and insignificant part of an arrow, but in relation to accuracy, it may be the most important component. Think of it this way: If the nock is not in perfect alignment with the arrow, then, as the string starts forward, it's driving the nock in one direction and the shaft in another. The result can be very poor accuracy. One day I was working on my form, shooting three-arrow groups with field points at 20 yards. On three straight groups, two of my arrows were dead center, and the third was off to the left a few inches. On the first two groups I thought my release was just bad on one arrow, but by the third group I knew it was the arrow, not me. So I checked nock alignment on that one arrow, and, sure enough, it was misaligned. Use a spin-tester or nock alignment tool to check nock straightness.

Nocks should snap lightly onto the string. If your nocks are too loose, you either need to use smaller nocks, or serve your bowstring with thicker serving thread to get a tighter nock fit. If they are too tight, do the opposite. A good test for nock fit is to nock an arrow and let it hang straight down from the string. When you thump the string, the arrow should fall off. If the arrow falls off under its own weight, the nock is too loose. If you cannot thump it off, it's too tight.

## Arrowheads

Point weight would be the first consideration here. Back in the old days, many traditional archers thought the heavier the better, and heads of 160 to 180 grains were not uncommon. With the advent of compound bows and the quest for speed, heads have gotten lighter and lighter until many archers now shoot heads as light as 65 grains.

Some people think head weight controls penetration, but it really doesn't. In relation to penetration, total arrow weight is what counts. Head weight has more relevance in relation to arrow balance. For an arrow to fly well it must be point heavy. To understand why, think of the hammer throw in the Olympics. Essentially the hammer is a steel ball on a chain. When the athlete spins and throws the hammer, the ball leads in flight with the chain trailing like a tail. If you simply threw a piece of chain with no ball, the chain would simply twirl around. The same principle applies to an arrow. For stability, the head must be heavier than the tail, and this is gauged by the balance point of the arrow. The amount of weight forward is debatable, but most experienced archers agree that a balance point 10 to 12 percent FOC (forward of center) is optimum.

To gauge FOC, first measure the total length of your arrow (with head installed) from the bottom of the nock slot to the point insert. Let's say that's 30 inches. Then, with a felt-tip pen, make a mark in the center of the arrow. In this case it would be 15 inches from each end. Now balance the shaft on a thin edge and make a mark at this balance point. You will see that this mark is forward of the center mark.

To compute FOC expressed as a percent, use this formula, where L equals the total length of the arrow in inches, and D equals the difference in inches between the two marks:

$$FOC\ \% = D/L$$

In other words, the center mark on a 30-inch arrow is 15 inches from each end. Let's say the balance point is 18 inches from the nock of the arrow. Thus, the difference (D) between these two marks is 3 inches. Divide 3 by the total length of the arrow (30 inches) and you get an FOC balance point of 10 percent. If the balance point is 19 inches from the nock, D equals 4 inches. Thus, when you divide 4 by 30, you get an FOC balance point of 13.3 percent.

*Field points (four, below right) are standard for general target practice. The Zwickey Judo (second from left) and Saunders Bludgeon (left) are also excellent heads for field practice and use in small game hunting.*

Choose heads that give you proper balance. This will depend on the weight of the shaft and the weight of the fletching. The heavier the shaft and the heavier the fletching, the heavier the head you'll need to achieve a 10 percent FOC.

Modern archers point out that ultrafast arrows are "critical" to shoot. That implies that arrow speed is the culprit. I suspect, however, that arrow balance has something to do with this. In order to achieve high arrow speeds, some archers will do anything to lighten their arrows, including shooting ultralight heads. In some cases their arrows probably do not have adequate FOC, and that's why the arrows are unstable in flight. Easton, the world's largest arrow maker, recommends an FOC for hunting arrows of 10 to 15 percent. And most experienced bowhunters insist on an FOC of 10 percent minimum.

**Practice Points:** For general practice, field points are the standard. They are accurate and easy on targets. The only guidelines are that all your points should weigh the same; they should weigh the same as the broadheads you'll hunt with; and they should be the same diameter as your arrow shafts (otherwise, they will destroy targets).

*Broadheads with a central column ferrule and three blades have proven most popular in the long run. Three 125-grain models I've used with excellent results are (from left) the Muzzy, Thunderhead, and Barrie Titanium.*

Other point styles are valuable for practice, as well. For stump shooting and random practice in the field, rubber blunts, like Saunders Bludgeons and Zwickey Judo Points are excellent. While hunting, I always keep an arrow tipped with either a blunt or a Judo in my quiver so I can take practice shots throughout the day. They're also excellent for collecting grouse and other small game. I prefer rubber blunts for small game, because they produce an immobilizing impact rather than shooting through small animals and birds.

**Broadheads:** According to archery collector Gene Hopkins, the first commercial broadhead was introduced in 1878 by the Peck & Snyder Company. To be sure, broadheads have come a long way since then, but they still serve the same purpose and must meet similar standards.

A first major consideration is durability. A few years ago, while hunting with outfitter Phil Phillips in Colorado, I shot an antelope, a relatively fragile animal, dead center in the chest. The result should have been double-lung penetration and a quick kill. Instead, the arrow penetrated only about an inch and fell out after the animal had taken only a couple of bounds. Phil and I followed that antelope for a couple of hours until dark, and we watched it through a spotting scope for five hours the next morning. We could see a blood spot on the antelope's chest, but some 15 hours after the shot, the buck was still going strong, obviously none the worse for wear, and we finally gave up the chase.

A couple of days later I killed a buck (with a different style of broadhead). As we butchered this animal, Phil and I boned out the shoulder blade and set it against a soft foam target. Then, using the same broadheads I'd shot into the first antelope, I took two shots into the shoulder blade. On the first, the tip of the head rolled into a "U" shape, and on the second the tip broke off — upon hitting the paper-thin shoulder blade of an antelope! Needless to say, I never used those fragile broadheads again.

Before using any heads, inspect the construction and blade-locking systems to make sure they're absolutely secure, and insist on blades at least .020 inch thick. Thinner blades can bend or break too easily. Then test the heads on an Ethafoam practice target or a foam 3-D target. If heads fail on targets, they could just as easily fail on animals. In general, heads with a center column surrounded by blades are more resistant to bending than flat heads. If you shoot a flat, two-edged blade, choose a welded model with a reinforced ferrule for strength. Some models with cutouts and only a narrow, unsupported blade, could fail on tough animals.

Accuracy ranks right up there with durability. If a broadhead doesn't hit in the right spot, it's just as useless as if it fell apart on impact. To start with, broadheads must be precision made. Before settling on a particular brand or style, mount several broadheads on your arrow shafts and spin each on the tip of the head. If you see any wobble where a head meets the shaft, the head (or shaft insert) is not straight. Buy only brands that spin true.

Then shoot them to test not only for durability but for accuracy. Just because they spin straight doesn't mean they'll hit in the same place as field points. The only way you can know is to practice with them. And if you're shooting open-on-impact heads, don't assume they necessarily fly like field points. Most do, but not all. Shoot them to make sure.

It's no accident that three-blade, replaceable-blade broadheads have gained major popularity over the years. Assuming they're well made, they will prove strong and accurate. The three brands I've shot most are Thunderhead, Barrie, and Muzzy, and all three have performed flawlessly. Other brands are equally good.

Through the 1980s and 1990s, such three-blade, replaceable-blade heads dominated the market, and they remain widely used today. In the late 1990s, however, open-on-impact broadheads grew in popularity, and continue to gain favor. The primary reason is accuracy. For the person who can't, or won't, make conventional broadheads fly straight, open-on-impact heads offer a welcome panacea. If a person can get field points to fly well, he can get most expandable heads to fly straight and group closely. This is particularly true with high-speed bows, say over 260 feet per second. Many archers agree that when arrows exceed that speed, getting fixed-blade heads to shoot with pinpoint accuracy can be difficult.

Large cutting width is another plus for open-on-impact heads. Whereas the average fixed-blade head has a cutting width of $1\frac{1}{8}$ to $1\frac{1}{4}$ inches wide, most expanding heads have widths, when opened, from $1\frac{1}{2}$ to 2 inches. One model expands to $2\frac{3}{4}$ inches wide. In addition, some people consider expanding heads safer than conventional heads, because the blades are

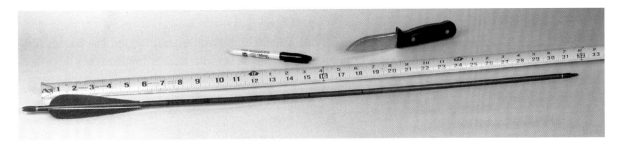

largely hidden within the body of the head until the arrow strikes a target.

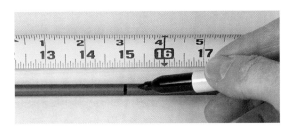

On the negative side, some hunters report lack of penetration as a problem. Many open-on-impact heads have severe blade angles that produce more of a chopping than a slicing action. That trait combined with wide cutting width definitely can restrict penetration. In addition, on angular shots, one blade can catch and open before the other blade makes contact, throwing the shaft off course and robbing it of energy and penetration.

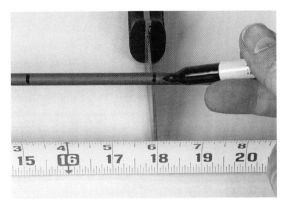

*Top:* Measure the total length of your arrow shaft from the low point of the nock groove to the cut end of the shaft. This arrow measures 30 inches long. The felt marker is to mark the arrow, and the knife is to use as a balance beam for the arrow.

*Middle:* Mark the exact center of the arrow with a felt marker. On this 30-inch shaft the center mark is at 15 inches.

*Bottom:* Balance the arrow on a thin edge (in this case a knife blade) and mark the point at which the arrow balances. This arrow balances 18 inches from the nock, or, three inches in front of the center of the shaft. 3 (inches FOC) divided by 30 (inches total arrow length) computes to a balance point of 10 percent FOC.

Lack of durability and dependability are other problems cited by some experienced bowhunters. A companion of mine shot a turkey with an open-on-impact head. Hitting the turkey's wing, the arrow fell to the ground, and the turkey flew away unscathed. One of the broadhead's blades was intact, one was twisted into a useless shape, and the third had broken off. I've had some brands self-destruct on targets, which doesn't encourage me to shoot them at big game.

Certainly many open-on-impact broadheads are excellent, and a lot of negative observations carried over from the early days of expandables when, frankly, some were junk. Designs and construction have improved greatly in recent years, and many open-on-impact heads these days are excellent. If you decide to hunt with open-on-impact heads, follow these guidelines:

1. Buy highest quality. Test heads on Ethafoam targets, and if a particular brand comes apart, don't hunt with it.
2. Analyze design. Expanding heads open in various ways, from direct pressure on the blades to elaborate plunger systems. Again, test these, and shun iffy systems that could fail to open.
3. Pick shots carefully. Stick to broadside shots so your arrow hits perpendicular to the target and all blades make contact at the same time.

4. Shoot adequate poundage. Expanding heads require more energy than conventional heads do for adequate penetration. While no one can prescribe an absolute minimum, I'll stick my neck out by recommending a minimum draw weight for compound bows of 60 pounds for deer and 70 for elk and other large animals.

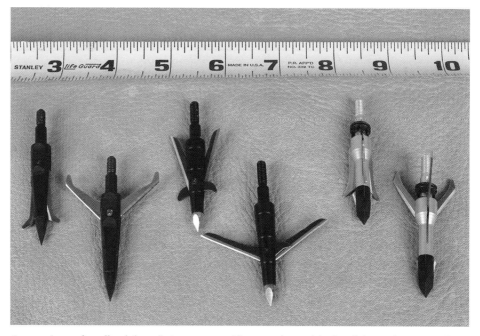

*Open-on-impact broadheads have their proponents. Three popular models, from left, are the NAP Spitfire, Barrie Gator, and Grim Reaper.*

Keep in mind that in some states, open-on-impact heads are illegal. In Oregon the regulations read: "Broadhead blades must be fixed..." In Idaho: "No person shall take big game animals: With ... expanding broadheads." Expanding heads are also illegal in Alabama, North Carolina, Rhode Island, and Ohio. Check in the states you hunt to make sure expanding heads are legal.

Remember, regularly check the blades on arrows in your quiver. On traditional-style heads, you can use a stone to sharpen the blades much as you would a knife, and you can do a quick touch-up with one of the hand-held sharpeners with opposing steels. These automatically put the right angle on the blade. On broadheads with replaceable blades, replace the blades occasionally. Never shoot a broadhead at an animal unless the blades are either new or are honed to a fine edge.

## Arrow Making

Making your own arrows is a fairly simple process. You can save money by making arrows, you can make them to your own specs, and you probably can make them better than most store-bought arrows.

To make arrows, you need: a fletching jig and clamps, fletching glue, rubbing alcohol, emery cloth, two-part epoxy or hot-melt glue, arrow cutoff saw, shafts, vanes or feathers, nocks, point inserts.

Note in particular the references to cleaning the shafts. If you clean the insides of the shafts before gluing inserts into place, you will never have an insert pull out. And if you clean the fletching areas well, fletching will last for years. Here are the essential steps:

1. Insert nocks. The nock wrench enclosed with these nocks makes this a simple process. If installed dry (without glue), you can later index them for maximum fletching clearance. If you decide to glue nocks into carbon arrows, use only rubber cement. Fletching glue can damage the shafts.

2. Cut shafts to length. Use only a high-speed rotary cutoff saw for this step. If you don't own a saw, take the shafts to a pro shop for cutting.

3. Chamfer and clean the insert ends of the shafts. Use a lightly abrasive tool like the one shown here, which was supplied with the shafts, to clean burrs from inside the shaft. Then use Q-Tips and rubbing alcohol to swab the inside of the shaft clean. Also wipe the inserts with alcohol.

4. Glue in inserts. On carbon shafts, use a two-part, 24-hour epoxy. Five-minute epoxy tends to be more brittle and will not hold up to impact as well. On aluminum arrows, you can use hot-melt glue.

5. Clean fletching area. Very lightly buff the fletching areas of each shaft with fine grit sandpaper or emery cloth. Then wipe the shafts clean with alcohol on a clean paper towel or clean rag.

6. Apply glue to fletching. Place a vane (or feather) in the fletching clamp and run a light bead of glue evenly along the base of the vane.

7. Apply fletching to shaft. Firmly seat a shaft in the fletching jig and solidly seat the clamp onto the jig so that the glue-covered base of the fletching makes full contact with the shaft.

8. Let glue dry. With fast-set glue, you need to wait only 10 seconds or so before applying the next vane. With conventional fletching glue, wait 10 to 15 minutes. The product is a finished arrow to your exact specs.

*Use a nock wrench, such as the one shown at the bottom of the photograph above, to install nocks on aluminum or carbon shafts.*

*When cutting shafts to length use only a high-speed rotary saw to guarantee that your cuts are at the proper angle.*

*The insert ends of the arrow shaft must be de-burred with an abrasive tool and carefully cleaned with rubbing alcohol before gluing or attaching the nock and point or broadhead.*

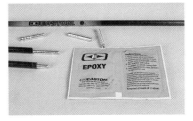

*Use a two-part epoxy cement to glue inserts on carbon shafts. On aluminum arrows, you can use hot-melt glue.*

*Chapter 4*

# Shooting

# A
ny modern bow is capable of tack-driving accuracy at virtually any distance. You could prove that by shooting the bow by machine, because unless the bow, arrows, or the shooting machine have structural flaws, the bow will stack arrows in a bull's-eye out to 100 yards. In very few cases, then, can you blame shooting deficiencies on the bow. It's you, the shooter, who is fouling things up, and that leads to the underlying principle behind good archery: Get out of the way and let the bow shoot the arrow. If you can do that, you've solved most shooting problems, and you will place arrows accurately and consistently.

## Relaxation

How do you get out of the way? In a word, you relax. The more relaxed you can remain during the shooting process, the less influence you will have on the bow, and the better the bow can perform. Every aspect of your shooting form should contribute to relaxation during the shot. Your bow hand is the key to relaxed shooting. Not only does it have a profound influence on the bow, but it's a barometer of relaxation and tension throughout your body. As goes your bow hand, so goes the rest of your body.

*To prepare for field conditions, practice shooting from your knees and other varied positions.*

To remain relaxed throughout the shot, your overall posture should be natural and comfortable, your face muscles should be free of all tension and strain, and the muscles of your arms and shoulders, even while holding the bow at full draw, should remain relaxed.

Over the years I've received instruction from several top-level archers and coaches, among them Lonnie Jones, a former professional coach; Jim Pickering, a champion archer and bowhunter; Randy Ulmer, a 3-D and target champion and highly successful hunter; and George Chapman, head instructor of the PSE Shooter School in Tucson, Arizona. All of them emphasize the need for relaxation during the shot.

They teach other common elements that apply to all archery and bowhunting as well. For the sake of clarity, I will discuss these elements in the context of the practice range. Then I will go into methods for adapting proper form to hunting conditions. Keep in mind one more thought — all principles of good archery apply to traditional bows just as they apply to compounds. (All directions are for right-handed shooters. Do the opposite if you're left-handed.)

## Stance

Accuracy always starts here, because stance is the platform for the rest of your body. Solid stance, steady sights; wobbly stance, wobbly sights. It's just that simple.

Start by facing 90 degrees to the target with your feet shoulder width apart and take about a half step back with your left foot to open your stance toward the target. Keep your feet shoulder width apart and keep your weight balanced evenly on both feet. Do not lean forward or back to place more weight on one foot or the other. Keep weight evenly distributed on both feet.

As you turn your head to look at the target, hold your neck and head in a natural, comfortable position, and maintain this position throughout the shot. You may have a tendency to lean your head to the side, forward, or back, to bring it to the string as you raise and draw your bow. Do not do that. Do not move your face to meet the string. Rather, bring the string to meet your face.

This is where correct draw length is so important. If the draw length of your bow is too short, you'll want to tip your head forward to meet the string; if it's too long, you'll want to tip your head back to see through the peep. With the right draw length, you can draw and aim the bow without moving your head. Again, don't fit your body to the bow; fit the bow to your body.

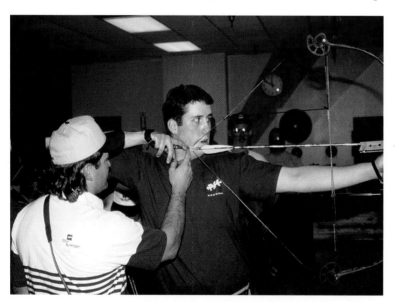

*To shoot accurately, you must get out of the way and let the bow shoot the arrow. The key to doing that is relaxation. At the PSE Shooter School, you learn to get out of the way so the bow alone can shoot the arrow.*

*A solid stand is the foundation for all good shooting. Start by facing 90 degrees to the target (above left). (Assume the camera is the target.) Then take a half step back with your front foot and turn slightly toward the target (above right), giving yourself a mildly open stance. Keep weight evenly distributed on both feet.*

## Hand Placement

If you spontaneously raise your arm and point at a distant object, you'll notice that your hand is angled diagonally. That's its natural position, and that's the position your hands should maintain when you're shooting a bow. Why? Because if you let your hands fall into that position, especially your bow hand, it is torque free. It will not twist the bow either way after the shot.

Place your left hand on the bow handle in this naturally rotated angle. You can check your hand position at full draw to see if it's right. If it is rotated correctly, the tip of your little finger will not be in front of the bow, but to the left of the bow handle.

The grip of the bow should be pressing only against the meaty part of your thumb. Some archers rotate the wrist upward so that the bow presses against the web between the thumb and the index finger. This is called a high-wrist position. That does minimize the amount of contact with the hand, which is good, but it is not the most stable position for the wrist. Most archers will do better by letting the wrist relax so that the grip of the bow presses snugly against the meaty part of the thumb in a medium or low-wrist position.

Throughout the shot, the fingers on your bow hand should remain loose and relaxed. You sometimes see archers with their fingers sticking out straight, like spokes on a wheel, or clutching the bow with a white-knuckle grip. Both of these are bad, because they're the result of tension. Remember, you want complete relaxation as you shoot your bow. Even at full draw, the fingers on your bow hand should remain loose and limp. And they should remain loose, even after the shot. Watch professional archers shooting targets, and you will see that they literally drop their bows after the shot. If you're keeping your bow hand limp throughout the shot, as you should, you also will drop your bow after every shot.

That's why it's so important to equip your bow with a wrist sling. Without the sling you must hold onto the bow during and after the shot, which forces you to grip the handle tightly — and forces the bow to do things it does not want to do. With the sling in place you can let your bow hand totally relax, and the bow can do its own thing during and after the shot.

## Shoulders and Arms

As you raise and draw the bow, keep your bow shoulder pulled low; this is the most stable position. Do not hunch your shoulder. If you cannot hold your shoulder down as you draw your bow, the draw weight of your bow is too heavy. For now you should lower the draw weight to a point at which you can hold your shoulder down. Exercises like pushups, pull-downs and seated rowing exercises will strengthen your shoulder and back muscles.

Allow the elbow on your bow arm to remain slightly bent throughout the shot. In this relaxed position it acts like a shock absorber and allows the bow to "float" in a natural position. If you straighten your arm into a rigid, straight post, you can force the bow to one side or the other.

Before you draw, check the fingers of your drawing hand. If you shoot with fingers or with a wrist-strap release aid with a rotating head, your hand should be in the same natural, rotated position as your bow hand. With some release aids, holding your hand that way is not possible, and your drawing hand may be held vertically or horizontally.

As you hold the bow at shoulder level in a pre-draw position, the elbow on your drawing arm should be held high, slightly above shoulder level. Then, draw by pulling your elbow down and around behind your head. The bulk of the work in drawing the string should be done with the large muscles of your upper back.

When you hit full draw, find a solid anchor point. This will vary, depending on your style of shooting, but it's critical to develop a positive, solid anchor point, because the anchor is equivalent to a rear sight. You can imagine how poorly you would shoot if you had a wobbly rear sight on a rifle. Your results in archery will be the same if you have a wobbly anchor.

Most fingers shooters anchor with the index finger in the corner of the mouth, although some who shoot barebow will anchor higher with the middle finger at the corner of the mouth. This is how I anchor when shooting traditional bows to bring the arrow closer to my aiming eye. Many target archers shooting with sights anchor by placing the thumb knuckle under the chin.

Shooting with a release aid, you have many anchoring options, and they may vary, depending on your style of release aid. Shooting with a back-tension release aid, I anchor with the big knuckle of my thumb planted just behind my jawbone near the bottom of my ear. Archers shooting release aids with rotating heads often turn their hands so that the back of the hand is pressed against the cheek. Find an anchor position comfortable for you, and work on it until it is solid and consistent.

A couple of anchor checks will help. The peep sight is an anchor confirmation. If you're anchored well, you should be looking directly through your peep sight. Many expert archers recommend touching the string to the tip of your nose at full draw as another anchor check.

## Releasing the String

A good string release can be summed up in one word — surprise! You never want to anticipate the release of the string. As you aim, the string should suddenly be gone. It's like squeezing the

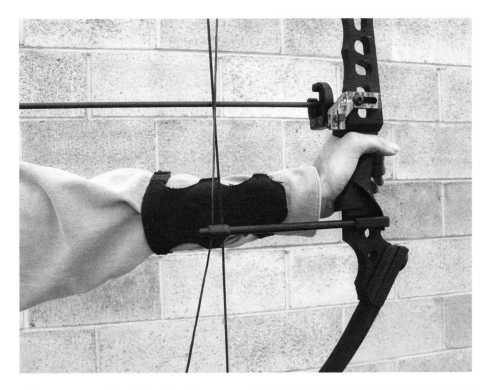

For most archers, a low-wrist position like this will prove most stable and consistent. As you can see, the handle is pressing primarily against the meaty part of the thumb. The wrist string has been removed for the purpose of clarity in this illustration.

trigger on a rifle. You simply start squeezing and the rifle goes off, startling you.

The bow hand is your barometer for relaxation. Your fingers should remain loose throughout the shot. If the hand is rotated correctly, the tip of your little finger should rest to the side of the bow.

The specifics may vary, depending on the method of release, but the principles and results should be the same, regardless. To get a surprise release, you want to continue pulling with your back as if you were continuing the draw. If you're shooting with fingers, just allow your hand to relax as you pull with your back muscles. At some point the fingers will relax to the point at which the string will pull away. Your hand should simply move straight back along your face after the release.

To get the feel, hold a bucket weighing 4 or 5 pounds by the bail. Place the bail across the first knuckles of your three shooting fingers as you would a bowstring, and hold the bucket a few inches above the ground. Let your hand slowly relax until the bail slips from your fingers. That's the way you should release the bowstring. As archery pro Lonnie Jones explained to me years ago, "Don't let go of the string. Let the string go." There's a huge difference, and that advice will serve you well. To get a good release with fingers, simply allow your drawing hand to relax — until the string slips away. Surprise!

With a release aid the principle is identical, but a surprise release is easier to achieve because you don't have direct contact with the string. With a trigger-finger release, you simply start squeezing the trigger slowly until the bow goes off. Rather than moving only your finger to trigger the release, pull with your back so that your entire hand is pulling into the release aid.

A back-tension release aid further increases the potential for surprise. With this style, you essentially pull with your back muscles to rotate the release aid until the string slips off a hook on the release aid (for more on this, see Beating Target Panic on page 68). This style assures the ultimate in a surprise release — and, thus, the ultimate in consistency and accuracy.

## Follow-Through

After the shot, you essentially keep doing what you were doing before you released the string. That's follow-through. That might sound like a no-brainer, but it isn't always easy, because the natural tendency is to drop your bow arm instantly to watch the arrow fly through the air and hit the target. That's the worst thing you can do, because you will start anticipating the shot and moving your bow before you release the string. The results will not be favorable.

To assure greatest accuracy, continue aiming at the target after releasing the string. Your bow arm may drop slightly under the weight of the bow. But it should drop only slightly, straight down. If it jerks to one side or the other, you probably have some serious muscle tension in your shoulder or arm. Also, analyze your stance. You may need to open or close it slightly. With proper alignment, your bow arm should move straight toward the target, not to the side.

Continue to hold the follow-through position until your arrow hits the target. If you're

*As you draw and hold your bow in shooting position, pull your bow shoulder low — do not hunch this shoulder — and allow your bow arm to remain in a slightly bent, relaxed position. Notice that in both of these photos, my feet are shoulder width apart and my weight is evenly distributed on both feet. I am standing in a natural, relaxed position, not leaning forward or back, and my head is upright in a natural position.*

shooting properly, you probably will not see your arrow in flight or hitting the target. Wait until you hear the impact before lowering your bow. A good way to perfect follow-through is to practice at long range. Stand 50 to 60 yards from the target butt, and after each shot continue to aim until you hear the arrow hit the target. If you can perfect your follow-through at those distances, you will have total control over it at closer ranges.

# Aiming

Here's one more point in shooting accuracy — accept the fact that you can never hold your sight pin absolutely steady. To some degree it will always float back and forth across the target. For beginners, the range of motion will be much greater than for experienced archers. Of course, you should strive to develop your strength, form, and relaxation to reduce this movement as much as possible. But don't try to solve the problem of sight movement by gritting your teeth and tensing your muscles in an attempt to hold that pin rock-solid on the bull's-eye. That will only aggravate the movement.

Even more critically, never try to time a shot by releasing the string quickly as your sight pin crosses the target. By the time you get rid of the string, the sight pin will be off-target again and your accuracy will only deteriorate — rapidly.

No, the secret to accuracy is to stay relaxed as you aim, letting the sight pin rove in its natural arc. As you're aiming this way, slowly begin to release — relax your fingers, squeeze the trigger, or apply back tension — until the bow goes off. Never try to time the shot, and don't hesitate or start over once you have begun your release. Simply execute the release smoothly as you continue to aim, and let the arrow fall where it may. It will consistently fall where you want it.

This is the closest thing to magic you will experience in archery, because it is a paradox: the harder you try to aim precisely, the worse you will shoot; the more you relax and let the sight wander, the better you will shoot. You don't believe me? Try it.

# Form Practice

I've heard archers say, "I can't shoot paper worth a darn, but I'm deadly on animals." Think about that. A person shooting paper is under no pressure, the weather is fine, he's rested, and his adrenaline level is normal. If he can't consistently hit the bull's-eye under those ideal conditions, how can he rationally expect to do better when gripped by stress, lousy weather, fatigue, and emotion? The fact is, a bad archer is a bad archer, regardless of circumstances, and his only hope in the field is luck, a poor substitute for shooting ability.

Some people advise against standing in front of a target butt, shooting arrow after arrow with perfect form, because that's not really like hunting. I could not agree less. Whether you shoot a stickbow instinctively or a compound with sights and a release aid, good form is the foundation for every shot. Certain elements of good form — relaxed bow hand and arm, solid stance, head position, in-line drawing arm, smooth release, follow-through — apply to every shot you'll ever take, whether you're standing on a tournament line or crouching under a spruce tree, drawing on an elk. So always be working on your form.

Equally important is repetition. If you practice only a couple of weeks before the season to check your sights, you might decide you're shooting quite well enough. But gripped by the adrenaline rush and excitement of tense hunting action, you'll probably forget every step of good shooting form you've ever learned and simply fling an arrow.

I vividly recall my first shot ever at a bull elk. He was 15 yards away, feeding, as I confident-

*Consistent, quality practice throughout the year will pay off in the long run. You don't need to practice at long range or under field conditions. I have a bean bag target in my shop where I can take a few shots at anytime, no matter how bad the weather, to work on my form.*

ly drew my 58-pound Kittredge recurve. Up to that point, everything was cool. But suddenly my mind went blank, and I launched an arrow about 3 feet over the bull's back.

Since then, I've killed my share of elk with well-placed arrows, but all of my shots have had one common element — I have never remembered shooting an arrow. My mind still blanks out. The only difference now is that I've practiced form so much that my mind and body go on autopilot, and things go right despite me. Something similar happens to most bowhunters. Few remain calm enough in the heat of battle to concentrate on shooting form. And that's the value of repetitious practice. It builds muscle and nerve memory, so that your body automatically performs well, even when your mind is blank.

The beauty of form practice is that you can do it almost anywhere. If you can safely shoot in your backyard, that's ideal, but it isn't necessary. You can place a target butt in your garage or basement. In the winter I hang a bean bag target in my shop and practice there. Although the distance is scarcely 10 feet, I can work on my form and shooting technique. Then when hunting season arrives, I have no doubts about my shooting or tackle.

Here's one last thought on form practice: When you're worried about hitting a target, your focus switches from shooting technique to shooting success, from process to results. To really progress as an archer, you must forget about where your arrows are hitting and focus strictly on execution of the shot. The best way to do that is to shoot with your eyes closed.

To prevent a disastrous miss, stand 10 feet or so from your target butt. Prepare for the shot as described, but when you come to full draw and are aiming at the target, close your eyes. Now run through a checklist of essential points: Is my stance balanced and solid? Bow hand limp? Anchor solid? Head in a natural, relaxed position? When everything checks out, begin your release. After the bow goes off, hold your follow-through for several seconds with your eyes closed and evaluate your form. Has my string hand moved straight back along my face? Am I still holding my bow in aiming position? Open your eyes only after you have checked your form thoroughly. Shoot several arrows this way each practice session to build good shooting habits.

## Quality Practice

Not long ago I visited Randy Ulmer, a top 3-D archer and hunter. During some friendly competition, I said, "Don't you let me beat you just to make me feel good."

"Not a chance," he laughed. His response revealed his competitive nature, but it also suggested a practice ethic. "I always shoot to the best of my ability," Ulmer explained. "My strongest practice philosophy is that I never shoot an arrow without a purpose. With each shot, I'm working on some aspect of my form — my bow hand, relaxation, aiming. If you practice mediocre shots, you'll be a mediocre archer. You don't have to practice a lot to do real well. If you practice shooting every arrow right, you'll develop the good habits needed to shoot well under any conditions."

Dave Holt, an archery instructor and technical editor for *Bowhunter* magazine, said, "Commonly, people who come to my archery school have to warm up first, and then they start shooting well. They might say, 'What do you think of that?' And I say, 'I'm not interested in your good arrows. I'm interested in your worst arrows.' A hunter may get only one shot — so that first shot must always count."

Finally, you need to practice throughout the year. With any extended layoff, you get stale. I would compare shooting a bow far more closely with a sport like golf than with rifle shooting, because results depend largely on human performance. A golfer, for example, must continually work on conditioning, form, timing and rhythm to maintain peak ability. Ditto archers. In my opinion, experienced bowhunters should practice a minimum of one month before the season, novices, two months or more. And year around is better.

If you alter tackle or form, devote even more time. Many years ago I changed my anchor point two weeks before the season, which didn't seem to be a problem since the new anchor came naturally. When shooting at a deer, however, I unconsciously reverted to my old anchor point — and missed the deer by several feet. If you plan to change anything, allow for three to four months' practice to ingrain new habits.

A bowhunter who puts his tackle away at the end of one season and takes it out just before the next is making a big mistake. Shooting any style of bow well requires consistent practice.

## Field Practice

This might sound contradictory, but now I will say you need varied practice. With the above steps, you will build the solid foundation of form mandatory for good archery. But you then need to adapt that form to the field, where conditions will rarely be perfect. In hunting, you will be shooting sharply upward and downward, kneeling or sitting, bending to shoot under obstacles. And you will be shooting in terrible weather conditions when the wind is blowing and snow is falling. And on top of all of this, you could be tired from hiking long miles, or stiff from sitting on stand for long hours.

To prepare for field conditions, practice shooting while sitting flat on the ground, kneeling, and shooting at steep angles. If you don't have any hills where you live, shoot from the roof of your house down onto the lawn. Remember to bend at the waist rather than just lowering your bow arm. You want to keep your alignment the same for every shot, regardless of angle. Vary your shooting speed, as well, sometimes drawing and shooting rapidly, other times drawing as slowly as possible and aiming for several seconds.

Not long ago, I read a story in which the author had practiced with field points all summer and then screwed broadheads onto his arrows just before the season. He'd never shot the broadheads. Then he expressed surprise that his first shot at a deer careened off target. The real surprise is that an editor would print such ignorance. But more to the point here, you can't assume broadheads will fly like field points, so practice with them — ahead of the season.

Practice in your hunting clothes, too. Huddled in a bulky coat, face mask, and heavy gloves on a frigid tree stand, you won't shoot as you do while practicing in shorts and a tank top. Don't wait until a buck stands broadside at 20 yards to discover the differences. Shooting only under pleasant conditions won't prepare you for hunting. Take advantage of any nasty day to get in some valuable practice. If you practice regularly during stormy weather, when you're tired, and from varied positions and angles, you will make tough hunting shots look easy.

You can do most of the above during regular practice sessions at home, but you should go further to adapt to hunting conditions. A good starting point is 3-D shooting, because the lifelike targets are placed at unmarked distances and the targets are commonly placed so that you have to shoot around obstacles, as you would in hunting. Competition also adds an element of pressure similar to what you might feel when you're drawing down on a trophy in the field.

Stump shooting, or roving, is just what the name implies — roving through the woods and fields, shooting at rotten stumps, pine cones, dirt clods, and other convenient targets. It also provides invaluable practice. Stump shooting includes most of the elements of hunting (except, perhaps, the pressure), and you can do it just about anywhere. All you need are some arrows equipped with Judo points or rubber blunts, and a little free time.

Above all, don't stop practicing when the season opens. It distresses me to hear guys on a hunt say they haven't shot an arrow in a week or 10 days. That borders on irresponsibility, because no one can lay off that long and be at peak form when a big game animal comes within range. On any extended hunt, include a practice target in your essential gear, so you can practice in camp.

In addition, I always carry a practice arrow tipped with a Judo point or rubber blunt in my quiver. Then, during any slack time I take some practice shots (or collect grouse or other small game for the pot). I consider that practice arrow the most valuable arrow in my quiver, because it keeps me sharp for the real thing. It also provides a constant tackle check. Over the years, I have discovered several problems with my bow, arrow, rest, and sights while shooting in the field. Regular shooting practice during the hunt should be part of every bowhunter's routine.

# Beating Target Panic

In August 1996, I sneaked up on a feeding mule deer and drew my bow confidently. This was a slam dunk. But when I shot, the arrow clattered off a rock 2 feet to the right of the deer, and the buck soon became a small cloud of dust disappearing over yon horizon. You could say I simply made a bad shot and that I should have practiced more before the hunt. But that would really not be an accurate conclusion.

In his book, *Balanced Bowhunting*, Dave Holt defines buck fever as "becoming so excited and/or wanting to succeed to such a high degree that mentally and physically you fail to perform to your full potential." That sums it up. I had missed not because I could not shoot well or because my bow wasn't sighted accurately, but because I wanted "to succeed to such a high degree" that my performance dropped well below my potential. In short, I got buck fever and blew it.

After 25 years of bowhunting, you'd think I would have been above such weakness, but that situation proves otherwise. Am I alone? Hardly. Beginning archers predictably suffer buck fever or shoot poorly and miss some shots, but veteran bowhunters can develop bad habits that just as surely hurt their performance.

As already discussed above, for maximum accuracy with a release aid, the shot must come as a total surprise. If you anticipate the shot, you will punch the trigger and your accuracy will suffer. That's what happened to me. I was shooting a release aid with an index-finger trigger, much like a rifle trigger, and I wanted to succeed so badly that the instant my sight came near the deer, I punched the trigger. "The index finger is very sensitive," Dave Holt explains. "You can feel when the release will go off, and you'll start punching the trigger."

How do you know if you're anticipating the shot and punching a release? One, you see your arrows flying to the target. That indicates you're dropping your bow hand to watch the arrow. And to do that, you must anticipate the shot. Bad habit. Also, you don't need a wrist sling to prevent dropping your bow, because you're anticipating the shot and grabbing your bow before it can jump out of your hand. Again, as stated numerous times above, your bow hand must remain relaxed throughout the shot. And if it does, the bow will fall out of your hand when you release the string. Again, use a wrist sling to catch it. Finally, you succumb to buck

*Further enhance the reality of practice sessions by shooting 3-D targets. Some 3-D practice will help my daughter Margie hone her archery skills.*

*By switching from a trigger-finger-style release aid to a Carter Revenger back-tension release aid, I was able to whip the worst symptoms of buck fever.*

fever and "fail to perform to your full potential." As a result, you spray arrows all over the target, and you miss easy shots on game.

Perhaps you think you can overcome target panic simply by trying harder, but you'll probably find that trying harder only makes the problem worse. You'll do far better seeking other solutions, and one common solution to target panic is purely mechanical.

Not long after missing that deer I was talking to Randy Ulmer. Hearing my story, Randy suggested I try a Carter Revenger, a release aid that has no trigger at all but is released by pulling with the back and rotating the wrist. This motion, using only large muscle groups, makes punching the release and shooting quickly nearly impossible. Initially, it took me 30 seconds or more to get the thing to fire. And when it did go off? Surprise! It about scared me to death. But soon I was releasing my shots in 5 to 10 seconds, longer than I'd ever before aimed in my life, and the results were astonishing. My groups were tighter than they'd ever been.

And my hunting success was proportional. I have continued to hunt with that back tension release aid, and it has proven very effective for me on animals. Missing shots as a result of buck fever has become a thing of the past, and my overall accuracy on big game has never been higher.

If you decide a back-tension release aid is not for you, try a release aid triggered by the little finger or thumb, which are less sensitive than the index finger and thus are less prone to jerking the trigger and causing errant shots. My daughter was punching the trigger badly on an index-finger release aid, so I switched her to a T-style release aid triggered with the little finger. This instantly cured her punching problem and she started shooting much better.

Other release aids are designed specifically to address target panic. The Answer, made by Golden Key-Futura absolutely will not fire if you jerk the trigger. If you squeeze the trigger slowly, the device will release the string; if you punch or jerk the trigger, it will not. You learn very quickly if you have a punching problem, and this style of release aid is an excellent training tool.

If you shoot with fingers, the solution for you might be a clicker. As the name implies, this device clicks as you reach full draw. The Clickety-Klicker and Cricket clickers have a clicking device that mounts to the inside of the upper bow limb and attaches to the bowstring with a fine cord. You adjust the cord to produce a click as you reach your correct draw length.

Clickers come in various styles to match your bow and shooting style, but they all work on the same principle — they signal when you should release the string. When you hear that click, your fingers spontaneously release the string. Because you do not know exactly when the clicker will go off, it creates an element of surprise very similar to that of a back-tension release aid.

Clickers are used primarily on traditional bows. If you observe target archers shooting recurve bows, you will see that all of them shoot with clickers. That's not happenstance. These precision archers know they will shoot best with the aid of a clicker, not only because the clicker creates a surprise release, but because it ensures precisely the same draw length each shot.

Earlier I talked about practicing with your eyes closed. Not only is this good for working on form but it's also a good way to overcome target panic. That's because target panic is largely a product of focus. That is, your focus switches from shooting well to hitting the target; from process to results. That's when you start punching the trigger, snap shooting, timing your shots, and any number of other bad habits. And they all happen because your whole focus is on hitting the target, whether that target is a paper bull's-eye or the lungs of an animal.

Shooting with your eyes closed transfers your focus from the target (results) to shot execution (process). If you do this enough, concentrating on executing a good shot each time you draw the bow, you can retrain your mind and body to function properly.

These are some basic ways to control and defeat target panic. If none of these work, I would suggest you go to a local pro shop or archery school to get some professional coaching. An unbiased observer can do wonders in restoring your enjoyment of archery. And enjoyment is what shooting a bow is all about.

*Specialized release aids can help cure target panic. At left, the Golden Key-Futura "The Answer" has a "can't punch" trigger. You must squeeze the trigger slowly and smoothly to release the string. If you punch the trigger, the release aid simply won't release. The Carter and Stanislawski back-tension release aids force you to continue to aim as you pull with the large muscles of your back. All of these devices are excellent training aids for overcoming target panic.*

*Chapter 5*

# Tune Up, Sight In

The route to shooting precision and skill is progressive. It starts with a good bow, includes quality accessories, and then requires solid shooting form. These are foundational.

But one step remains, and that's bow tuning, a buzzword among modern bowhunters and archers. While tuning can seem a little complicated and obscure, it's really a simple concept and process, similar to tuning a car, musical instrument, or any other mechanical device. Tuning involves getting all the parts of a device to work in harmony with each other for best possible performance. And so it is with a bow. Tuning is the process of adjusting the arrow rest, bowstring, cams, sights, and arrows to get the most out of your tackle.

## Initial Setup

As a starting point, adjust your arrow rest so the arrow is directly in line with the string. To do this, nock an arrow, hold the bow at arm's length in front of you, and line up the string with the center of the limbs. This would be called centering the string.

*On a hard hunt like this in Alaska, the hunter is protected by raingear, and all other gear is stowed safely inside waterproof bags. But the bow absorbs the full force of the weather. Keep it clean and lubricate the axles to ensure top performance.*

With the string centered, look past the string to the tip of the arrow. If the arrow tip lies to the left of the string, move the arrow rest to the right to bring the arrow into line with the string. If the arrow tip lies to the right of the string, move the rest to the left to bring the arrow into line with the string. In short, the string, center line of the bow, and the arrow should all be in line.

You can buy tools — the Golden Key-Futura Tru-Center Gauge, for example — made specifically for the purpose of centering the arrow. You place the base of the Tru-Center Gauge against the riser of your bow, swing the L-shaped arm around to the bowstring, and slide the marker on the arm to mark the exact position of the string. You then nock an arrow and swing the arm out in front of the bow and adjust the arrow rest until the arrow sits directly under the marker. The arrow is now in line with the string.

Now, with the arrow still nocked, look at the bow from the side. If you shoot with a release aid, start with the arrow at 90 degrees to the string. If the arrow runs parallel to the bow shelf, it should be about 90 degrees to the string. You can eyeball it, or to be more precise, you can use a small wood square or any object with a 90-degree angle. Hold one edge against the string and slide the 90-degree edge up close to the arrow. Ideally, the arrow will parallel the edge of the square. If it does, you're set to move to the next step. If the arrow is tail high, you can either lower the nocking point or raise the arrow rest. If the arrow is tail low, you can either raise the nocking point or lower the rest. However you accomplish it, if you shoot with a release aid, you want the arrow 90 degrees to the string.

If you shoot with fingers, line the arrow up as described above, but rather than setting it 90 degrees to the string, raise the nocking point one-quarter to one-half inch above 90 degrees.

Finally, before proceeding with tuning, check one last setting — fletching clearance. If fletching hits the arrow rest at any point, it can throw your arrow into wobbling flight. That's particularly true if your arrows are fletched with plastic vanes, because the relatively inflexible vanes deflect off the rest. Feathers are more forgiving because they collapse upon contact. Some hunters shoot feathers for that very reason — the feathers forgive tuning errors.

To assess fletching clearance, sight down the arrow as you did when centering your arrow with the string, and evaluate the position of the fletching in relation to the arrow rest. With a shoot-through rest, one of the vanes (or feathers) must pass through the support arms on the rest. You can tell simply by sighting down the arrow whether this "cock" vane will slide smoothly between the arms. If it appears a vane will hit any part of the rest, rotate the nock on the arrow until the vanes align with the openings between the rest arms. Here's where "tunable" nocks are valuable, because you can twist them to achieve maximum fletching clearance. Obviously, if you're using a drop-away rest, or a full-containment rest like the Whisker Biscuit, this guideline does not apply.

If you shoot with fingers, the fletchings must sweep out around the arrow rest. Again, sight down the arrow, and align the fletchings so they have the best potential to clear the rest.

## Paper Tuning

You hear a lot about paper tuning, which suggests that shooting an arrow through paper is a way to tune your bow. Really that's a misconception, because shooting through paper has nothing to do with actual tuning of the bow. Tuning involves adjusting the arrow rest, nocking point, arrow construction, and other variables. And in order to make the proper adjustments, you must be able to read your arrows in flight.

If you're rich, you can buy a high-speed camera and film your arrows traveling off the bow.

In an earlier chapter I mentioned my participation in one of Easton's high-speed filming sessions. In order to observe arrows in flight, Easton used a camera powered with a three horsepower motor that shot film at the rate of 7,000 frames per second. With this camera, Easton filmed arrows as they passed across the arrow rest. When the film is played back at normal speed, you can see in slow motion how arrows fly in response to different setups.

Most of us are not in that league, so we need a simpler and cheaper method. That's where shooting through paper comes in. Consider shooting through paper the poor man's version of slow-motion video.

*A simple device like the Golden Key-Futura Tru-Center Gauge helps you to center the arrow precisely. You set the block of the gauge against a flat part of the riser of your bow and set the mark on the L-shaped arm in line with the string.*

To shoot through paper, you need some kind of frame to hold the paper. Saunders makes an inexpensive portable frame just the right size for a single sheet of newspaper. Fancier paper tuners hold a roll of paper, so you can just keep rolling unblemished paper into the shooting frame.

Make sure the paper is tight on the frame, then place the paper in front of your target butt, stand about 10 feet from the paper, and shoot an arrow through the paper. Now analyze the tear in the paper. You will be able to see where the head hits first and the tail follows through the paper. The fletching cuts will be fairly obvious. From this you

*You then move the L-shaped arm in front of the bow and adjust the arrow rest until the arrow lines up with the mark. This arrow is not in line with the string.*

can tell if the arrow is flying tail right, left, high, low — or straight.

Ideally the arrow will be flying straight. If it is, move back and shoot a few more shots through the paper at various distances out to 20 yards. If your arrows are consistently going straight through the paper, sight in your bow (as described below) and go hunting. Your bow is on.

But what if the arrows do not fly straight? You should make some adjustments to get the best possible arrow flight. The whole idea of tuning is to bring the point end and nock end of the arrow into line so that the arrow is flying straight. Now here's the underlying principle for doing that: If you shoot with a release aid, you adjust the tail end of the arrow to bring it into line with the point. If you shoot with fingers, you

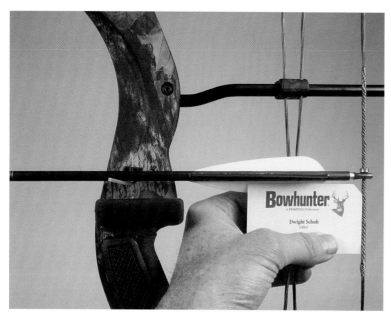

*Shooting with a release aid, you want the arrow set perpendicular (90 degrees) to the string. You can gauge this with a business card or square with a 90-degree angle. Notice that the arrow also parallels the bow shelf. On many bows, you can use the bow shelf to eyeball the arrow fairly close to 90 degrees to the string.*

*On shoot-through rests with two prongs or blades, sight down the arrow to line up the cock vane (or feather) with the gap between the support arms. If the cock vane does not line up properly, rotate the nock on the arrow to line up the vanes for maximum clearance.*

adjust the head end of the arrow to bring it into line with the tail.

Here's why: When you release an arrow with a release aid, the arrow essentially slides for its full length in contact with the arrow rest. Thus, the fletching end of the arrow is the last part of the arrow in contact with the arrow rest, and it's the part that will be most influenced by the rest. Thus, when shooting with a release aid, you tune for the back (nock end) of the arrow to bring it into line with the point.

In contrast, when you release the string with your fingers, only the first 5 or 6 inches of the arrow remain in contact with the rest. The arrow then flexes out around the rest and is free-flying well before the fletching and nock clear the bow. Thus, to alter the flight of the arrow, you must tune the front of the arrow to bring it into line with the tail. On a fingers-shot arrow, the rest essentially has no influence over the tail of the arrow.

With that concept in mind, let's look at specifics, first for the release aid (for a right-handed shooter). If the arrow is flying tail left, you could do one of two things: 1) If your rest has an adjustable side plate or plunger, you could reduce spring tension on the side plate, which would allow the tail of the arrow to move to the right into line with the point. 2) If your rest has no lateral tension adjustment, you can move the entire rest slightly to the right to bring the tail into line with the point. If the arrow is flying tail right, you would do the opposite: 1) Increase side-plate tension; 2) Move the arrow rest to the left.

If an arrow shot with a release aid flies tail high, you could: 1) Reduce spring tension of the arrow rest to allow the tail to drop into line with the point; 2) Lower the nocking point or raise the arrow rest to bring the tail into line with the point. If it flies low, you would do the opposite.

*Consider shooting through paper the poor man's version of slow-motion video. To shoot through paper, you need some kind of frame to hold the paper. Fancy ones like this hold a roll of paper so you can just keep rolling unblemished paper into the shooting frame.*

Now, if you're shooting with fingers, you would do just the opposite as you would with a release aid. If the arrow is flying tail left, you would: 1) Increase spring tension of the side plate to push the point into line with the tail; 2) Move the entire rest to the left to move the point into line with the tail. Again, if the arrow flies tail right: 1) Reduce side-plate tension; 2) Move the rest to the right.

If a fingers-shot arrow flies tail high, you could: 1) Increase support tension of the rest to hold the point of the arrow up in line with the tail; 2) Raise the rest or lower the nocking point to bring the point and tail into the same plane.

When tuning your bow, make only one adjustment at a time. If you change two or three things at once, you can't tell which is having a positive effect and which may impart a negative effect. So make one change, shoot two or three arrows through paper to judge the effect, and then make any needed adjustments.

Keep in mind, too, that your arrows don't necessarily have to shoot perfect bullet holes through paper to produce top accuracy. For one thing, as discussed in other sections of this book, arrows always oscillate to some degree when shot. Tears through paper will reveal this oscillation. So you could get neurotic trying to shoot perfect holes through paper at all distances when, in fact, that would be impossible because you cannot eliminate oscillation of the shafts.

If your arrows are tearing holes in paper no more than a half-inch long, you have a well-tuned bow and are more than ready for hunting. Try for perfection if you want, but don't give

up archery if you can't achieve it. You should be more concerned about shooting tight groups than you are about shooting perfect bullet holes through paper.

Finally, bear in mind that bow tuning is not an exact science. Far too many variables enter into the picture for anyone to guarantee absolute results. In regard to bow tuning, one size does not necessarily fit all.

## Other Thoughts

If your arrows are matched to your bow, the above steps will lead to the desired results. If they do not, you may have a fundamental problem that needs correction before you can get any tuning efforts at all to work. If you go through all of the above procedures and you simply cannot get your arrows to fly well, you should consult an arrow spine chart or a pro shop to evaluate your bow/arrow combination. If your arrows are grossly under- or over-spined for your bow, you may never get them to fly well. Spine is more critical for fingers shooters, but arrows must match any bow for good performance.

*Saunders makes an inexpensive portable, paper-tuning frame. made to hold a single sheet of newspaper. You can see that the upper tears were made by arrows flying grossly tail high and slightly right.*

If you're sure the arrows are spined correctly for your bow, and they still fly badly, you may need to look deeper. If you shoot a two-cam bow, rather than a single cam, the cams could be out of synchronization. That is, if one cam rolls over before the other during the shot, it will jerk the string violently up and down, imparting excessive oscillation into the arrow. The process of synchronizing cams is beyond the scope of this book. If you think that is the problem, take your bow to a pro shop for evaluation.

Some newer bows have synchronization marks on the cams. If that's the case, you can synchronize the wheels fairly easily yourself, although you may need a bow press in order to relax the bow so that you can remove and twist the cables. On bows with split-yoke cables, you can lift off and twist one side of the cable at a time to shorten or lengthen the cable.

Fletching contact could be the source of bad arrow flight. Even though you have

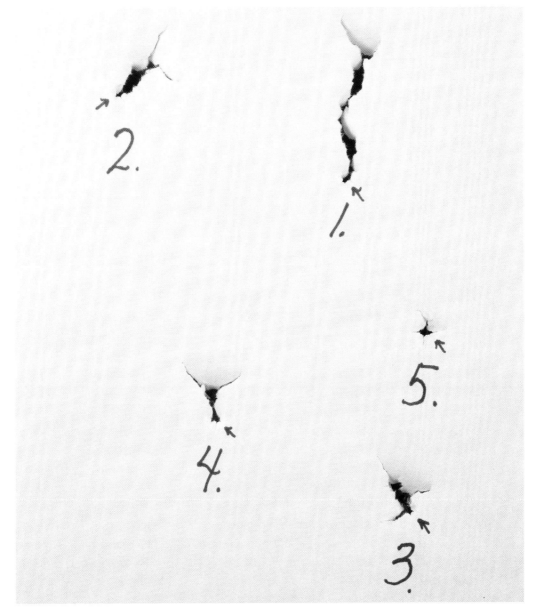

In this photo, the red arrows mark where the point of the arrow hit. When shooting with a release aid, adjust according to the following results. Tear **No. 1** is grossly tail high. Lower the rest or decrease vertical spring tension to improve this tear. **No. 2** is tail high and right. Reduce vertical tension and increase side-plate tension. **No. 3** is tail high and left. Again, reduce vertical tension but decrease side-plate tension. **No. 4** is slightly tail high. This tear is acceptable. **No. 5** shows a perfect bullet hole. Install broadheads and go hunting.

lined up the fletchings with the arrow rest, you might still have some fletching contact. To gauge contact, spray the bow shelf and rest, as well as the tail end and fletchings of your arrow with spray-on foot powder or deodorant. It should make a fine, unbroken, powdery film on the shaft and fletchings. Now shoot the arrow into your target butt and examine the powder for any places on the arrow or bow where the powder has been wiped away. You should be able to detect any signs of excessive or abnormal contact between the arrow and the bow or rest. Adjust your rest and nocks to eliminate this contact.

If the aberrations in arrow flight are consistent — that is, if the arrows always fly tail high,

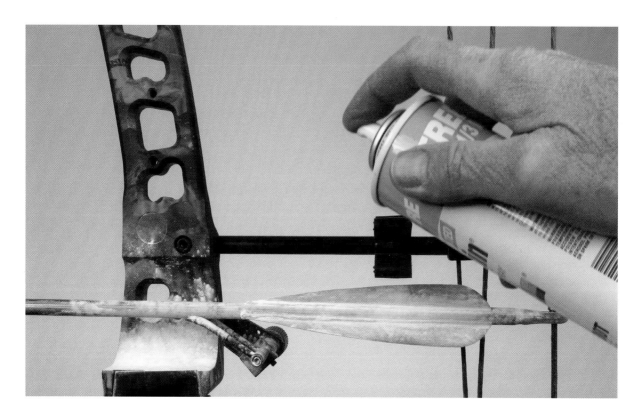

*To gauge contact, spray or dust the bow shelf and rest, as well as the tail end and fletchings of your arrow with spray-on foot powder or deodorant. It should make a fine, unbroken, powdery film on the shaft and fletchings. You can read excessive contact in the powder.*

or tail left — then the problem is probably mechanical. If the aberrations are inconsistent — that is, tail left one shot, tail right the next — the problem could very well be you and your shooting form. Any variations in hand placement clearly will alter arrow flight.

If you don't believe me, change your hand position on the bow and shoot through paper. You can "walk" the arrow from tail left flight to tail right simply by changing the angle of hand pressure on the bow handle. To iron out problems with form, review Chapter 4. Above all, place your hand on the bow the same way every shot, and keep that hand relaxed. In this sense, shooting through paper is a good diagnostic test of your shooting form.

## Sighting In

Before setting your bowsight, make sure your peep sight is set correctly. To check this, close your eyes, draw your bow, and settle into a solid anchor. Now open your eyes. You should be looking directly through the peep. If you are not, adjust the peep up or down the string as needed and repeat the eyes-closed process until the peep falls perfectly in front of your eye every time you draw. Do not tip your head forward or back to see through the peep. With the peep in place, you're ready to set the sight pins on your bowsight.

The method you use depends to some extent on the style of sight you shoot. But the principle is the same for all sights. For the sake of discussion here, let's assume you have a four-pin sight and want to set your pins for 20, 30, 40, and 50 yards.

Start by setting your 20-yard (top) pin. Stand 20 yards from your target butt and shoot three arrows at the bull's-eye. Don't worry whether the arrows hit the bull's-eye. They probably won't. For sighting in your bow, your only concern at this point is to shoot a tight group. Through the process of sighting in you will pull your groups into the bull's-eye.

Now, assuming you have shot a tight three-arrow group, here's the principle for setting your bowsight: You move your sight pin to the point of impact. Thus, if your arrows group low, you move the sight pin down; if they group high, move the pin up. If the arrows group left, move the pin left; if right, right.

After shooting your first group, move the sight pin in the appropriate direction. Shoot another group, and, if necessary, move the sight again. After three or four groups, you should be able to dial your 20-yard groups right into the bull's-eye.

With the 20-yard pin set, move back to 50 yards and repeat the same process for your bottom (50-yard) pin.

With those two pins sighted in, you can eyeball your 30- and 40-yard pins into position by spacing them evenly between the 20- and 50-yard pins. The distance between these pins will be slightly graduated, getting greater at the longer distances. With all of your pins set, shoot a few arrows at each distance to double-check your settings.

Changing the strings or cables on your bow could change the point of impact slightly. As long as you don't change the draw weight, you can simply use the gang adjustment on your bowsight to move all the pins in tandem to bring them back on target. Also, with experience you might find your peep isn't perfectly placed and will move it slightly up or down the string to make sighting easier. You then will need to reset your sight pins. Again, move all the sight pins at once with the gang adjustment.

Any modifications, such as changing draw weight or arrow weight, that change arrow speed, require that you readjust your sight pins individually, because spacing between the pins will be different.

## Shoot Your Broadheads

The final step in tuning and sighting your bow is shooting broadheads. If your arrows are tuned to shoot bullet holes through paper, chances are good that your fixed-blade broadheads will hit in the same place as your field points. And open-on-impact broadheads are likely to hit with your field points, even if arrow flight is not perfect.

But you can never assume that broadheads and field points will group in exactly the same place. If your arrows do not launch perfectly straight, the broadheads could cause a slight planing effect. For example, if the arrows fly tail high, they will plane low. If they fly tail right, they will plane left, and so forth. And you simply cannot gauge this without shooting them.

Shoot several three-arrow groups at 20, 30, and 40 yards. Your groups should be nearly as tight as they are with field points. If they are not, check the alignment of your broadheads to make sure they're well constructed and straight on the shafts. That's your first concern: tight groups.

If broadhead groups are tight — and are hitting exactly with your field points — you're ready to go hunting. But what if tight broadhead groups do not align perfectly with field point groups? Some veteran bowhunters might not agree with this, but I would say don't sweat it. The beauty of shooting with sights is that you can easily move groups simply by moving your sight pins. Most quality sights have a gang adjustment. With this feature, you should be able to move the entire sight to bring your broadhead groups dead center into the bull's-eye.

One last point: Never use your practice broadheads for hunting. Even one or two shots into

a target will dull the blades. At the very least you should replace the blades with fresh, factory-sharpened blades. But I would recommend that you designate several broadhead-tipped arrows for sighting in and practice and then use only brand-new arrows and broadheads for hunting big game.

## Tuning Your Stickbow

General principles for tuning stickbows are similar to those for compounds, but the process is somewhat simpler. If you shoot off the shelf, the only variables you can alter are arrow spine, nocking point height, and brace height.

Again, matching arrow spine to the draw weight of your bow is critical when shooting a stickbow because the bow most likely is not cut to center and is not equipped with a forgiving, adjustable rest, as most compounds are. Thus, you cannot adjust the "tune" of the arrow by changing the resistance or the position of the arrow rest. In addition, you most likely are shooting barebow, which means you cannot move groups onto the bull's-eye just by moving your sights, a luxury you have with any sighted bow. Rather, the arrows must hit where you are looking. To do that, they must be perfectly matched to your bow.

If you follow recommendations on the Easton arrow spine chart, or spine charts for other shafts, you may be right on target. Shoot a few arrows to see if they hit where you are aiming.

You can fine-tune your selection more closely, however, by shooting bare shafts. Select several shafts of various spine weights. Equip them with nocks and field points, but do not fletch them. Stand 15 to 20 feet from your target butt and shoot the bare shafts, aiming for the bull's-eye. You should soon detect a pattern. Some bare shafts will hit to the right of the bull's-eye, some will hit left, and others, you hope, hit dead center. Those that hit to the right are too weak in spine; those that hit to the left are too stiff; and those that hit in the center are just right. Fletch up a batch of the shafts that hit on target, and you're ready to proceed with finishing up your tuning.

To get the best arrow flight and to change the vertical impact of your arrows, move the nocking point up or down. Most stickbows shoot best with a nocking point placed so that a nocked arrow sits one-quarter to one-half inch above perpendicular (90 degrees) on the string.

The other adjustment you can make is brace height. Historically, longbow shooters used a measurement called fistmele to gauge brace height. This would be roughly 7 inches for most men. On most modern recurves, brace height falls somewhere between 7 and 9 inches. You can make subtle changes in brace height by twisting the string. To increase brace height, twist the string tighter; to lower brace height, untwist the string. The ideal brace height is the point at which the arrows fly best and the bow shoots most quietly.

# In the Field

Tuning and sighting are not one-time processes. A bow could be viewed as a living organism, and unbeknownst to you, things can change. Thus, you're wise to constantly check the tune and sights of your bow during a hunt. That's one reason for carrying a practice arrow in your quiver — if you shoot regularly, you will quickly spot abnormalities.

Many things can happen to alter your accuracy. While synthetic strings and cables have improved greatly over the years, they are not infallible, and over time, and particularly with greatly varying temperatures, they can change in length. Even a slight length change can significantly alter arrow speed — and impact point.

A peep sight, even if tied in securely, can slide up or down the string. When I climbed into my bear stand one evening, I shot my practice arrow tipped with a rubber blunt just to warm up and check my sights. The arrow hit low. That seemed strange to me, so I got down and moved away from my stand to shoot additional shots. They all hit low. Upon close inspection I could see that my peep sight had slid down the string slightly. Apparently I had caught it in the brush on my way to the stand and jerked it a fraction of an inch down the string. If I had not discovered this defect with a practice shot, I could have unwittingly missed or made a bad shot on a bear.

Other aberrations could affect accuracy equally or worse. Anytime you drop your bow or fight your way through brush with it, check the arrow rest. If the support arms on a rest get bent even slightly, impact point of your arrows will change significantly.

The same can be said of a bowsight. On one hunt, my practice arrows were consistently hitting 6 inches to the left of the target at 20 yards. I might not be the greatest shot in the world, but I'm not that bad. So I inspected my bow and discovered the aluminum sight bracket had got bent, moving all my sight pins to the right. I bent the sight back to the left and brought my arrows right back on target. But after that hunt I switched sights. If the flat aluminum sight bracket was going to bend that easily, I could not trust it on a hard hunt.

One other thing you should check regularly is lubrication on the cam axles. Before I went to Alaska in 1993, my 60-pound bow shot 450-grain arrows at 247 feet per second (fps). When I returned three rainy, muddy weeks later, draw weight had increased to 63 pounds and arrow speed had dropped to 239 fps. I had not oiled the axles and wheels in the field, but surely lubrication couldn't make that much difference. Could it?

To find out, I oiled the axles. Within a few shots, draw weight and arrow speed had returned to the original specs. While the need for lubrication can vary by bow, depending on the kinds of bushings or bearings used, this is one thing you always need to check, particularly on prolonged hunts in bad weather.

That knowledge proved valuable to me a couple of years later. While shooting some practice arrows on a sheep hunt in the backcountry of Idaho, I noticed my arrows were hitting consistently low. Remembering the Alaskan experience, I lubricated the axles on my bow. Voila! Almost instantly the arrows were right back on target. Clearly, little details can make a big difference in how your bow shoots — and in the outcome of a hunt.

*Chapter 6*

# Hunting Gear

The first half of this book addresses primarily the archery aspect of the bow-hunting equation, and by now you should have your tackle, accessories, and shooting technique pretty well under control. Logically, this second half addresses specifically the hunting aspect of the equation. And, as is the case with archery tackle, the obvious starting point is outfitting yourself with the right equipment.

Indeed, the right gear for the field plays just as large a part in your hunting success as does your archery tackle and shooting ability. Clothing, footwear, daypack, and other hunting accessories not only contribute to your stealth, but to your comfort, safety, and endurance. Because conditions vary so greatly by region, species, and hunting method, I can't prescribe a list of gear that covers all bowhunting. But I can give you a foundation that will cover the range of hunting conditions encountered by average, serious bowhunters.

*Take special pains to camouflage your face. For tree stand hunting, a cloth face mask is ideal. Rather than a loose mask, I personally prefer a full hood with elastic around the back of my head. This model, incorporated into a billed cap, is made by Scent-Lok.*

# Clothing, Footwear, etc.

***Silence:*** In bowhunting, perhaps more than in any other outdoors pursuit, clothes do make the man, not only because they have to keep you warm and comfortable under the extremes of conditions, but because they must be quiet when you're within 10 to 20 yards of the radar-acute senses of big game animals. The slightest whisper of clothing at those close ranges will produce much disappointment. Your success as a bowhunter will be only as good as your clothing.

In choosing clothing, silence is the most basic quality. In bowhunting, by very definition, you must function within the acute sensory range of animals, and noisy materials will not do. I clearly recall my first hunt for caribou in Quebec. In the rainy, windy weather, my guide wore raingear all day, which was understandable given the weather. The problem was that his raingear was made of nylon, and the pants zipped and zinged like .22 bullets ricocheting through the knee-high brush. Not only was the sound driving me nuts, but it alerted a number of caribou at distances as far as 100 yards away. My fleece raingear while not perfect, allowed me to move quietly enough to get within bow range of several bull caribou.

That's an extreme example, but the principle applies in all bowhunting, including stand hunting. On a calm day, a deer or bear 20 to 30 yards away will hear the slightest rustle of clothing as you turn your head or raise your arms to draw your bow. You must be able to make such subtle movements with absolute silence, and to do that your clothes must be whisper quiet.

Well-worn, soft cotton will work okay, and in warm weather, it's probably the first choice among many bowhunters. But it is never the best choice. Knit fabrics of wool, acrylic, or poly-

*To get close shots at animals, your clothing must be absolutely silent. On this Quebec caribou hunt, I had to escape my guide, who was wearing noisy nylon raingear, to get close to this bull. Here, I'm wearing knit clothing and a PolarFleece orange vest for totally silent movement.*

ester are softer and quieter, and equally good are synthetic fleeces — micro versions for warmer weather and full-nap versions for cold weather. Various polyester products such as Thermax and Cabela's Microtex are excellent for silent bowhunting, and the old standby, wool, is still one of the quietest materials available. Wearing clothes made of these materials, you can move and draw your bow on close-range animals without attracting attention (assuming your bow and arrow rest are equally silent). As already suggested, avoid clothes made of denim, nylon, and heavy cotton with a hard finish. These materials will cost you shots at some point.

Never ignore your extremities. For most of my hunting, I wear wool gloves that allow me to use my hands silently. In many situations I prefer knit or fleece caps to stiff cotton caps for the same reason. Even a twig grating across a cotton cap can alert a nearby game animal.

I will talk more about warmth below, but essentially you can achieve warmth in one of two ways — heavy insulation in a single garment, or layers of lighter clothing. I have found that shirts and jackets with heavy linings often bind and make a stretching sound as you draw your bow. Several layers of light garments allow more freedom of movement and are, thus, quieter.

**Concealment:** People commonly ask me which camouflage pattern they should wear in a certain area. The question often goes like this: "I will be hunting elk in central Idaho this fall. Can you recommend the best camo for that area?" Unfortunately, no one can give an absolute answer, but my personal opinion is that camo pattern is not a huge concern. Modern camo patterns look great, and they all work, but I suspect most are designed to hook buyers more than they are to fool deer.

More important than the precise pattern is the overall hue. This concept was made very clear to me while hunting the marshes at Sand Lake National Wildlife Refuge in South Dakota. Predator Gray was the lightest camo pattern I had, and it still was too dark in the yellow reeds and cattails. I stood out as a dark silhouette against the light vegetation, and deer were seeing me readily. One morning I was sitting on stand in the marsh when I saw a buck crossing an opening. Suddenly an arrow flew from the reeds, and the buck went down. I was impressed, because I had not seen the hunter, even though he was no more than 100 yards from me. So I walked over to congratulate him, and what immediately caught my eye was his marsh camo — faded tan Carhart overalls and jacket. Even with no camo pattern at all, the light tan clothes blended in beautifully with the yellowish marsh vegetation.

In open, environments — deserts or prairies for mule deer and antelope, the alpine for bighorn sheep, tundra for caribou — wearing camo that is too dark is the major sin. In the sagebrush of Nevada, for example, a hunter in a dark, forest camo will stand out as a distinct, black blob. Light patterns like Sage Country, Everywear West, Predator Gray, ASAT, or standard military desert camo blend in far better with light-colored surroundings. Amid the white trunks of aspen trees, or silhouetted in a tree stand against a bright, cloudy sky, a light, "sky" pattern often conceals you most effectively. On snow, a white snow pattern can work like magic.

At the opposite extreme, hunting in dark, shadowed woods, say for whitetails in an evergreen forest or elk or moose in the spruce woods, you want a fairly dark pattern, something like Mossy Oak Breakup, Realtree, or Trebark. In open hardwoods, a medium-hue pattern like Advantage is hard to beat. But, again, the main concern is hue. Back in my early days of elk hunting I wore nothing but plaid green wool, and elk didn't see me any more often than they do now as I wear the most sophisticated commercial camo patterns.

That's partly because movement, not pattern, is what really catches an animal's eye. That fact was reinforced in my mind by an incident in Montana, a state that requires all hunters to wear blaze orange during any firearms season. Thus, even though hunting with my bow, I was decked out in blaze orange vest and hat while creeping along a blocked-off logging road during Montana's late rifle deer season. When I spotted a whitetail buck feeding at the side of the road, I stood motionless as the deer fed my way. Even as I stood in the open, wearing blaze orange, the buck fed within 10 yards of me and did not spot me — until I moved. Then he caught me instantly and bounded away.

To complete any concealment system, take special pains with your face and hands. Your face is the one part of your body that will always be in view of an animal, and most people's skin, whether light or dark, will shine and stand out. Many hunters wear cloth face masks of one kind or another, which range from lightweight netting to heavyweight fleece. I

This light-colored Predator camouflage blends well with the white trunks of aspen trees. In warm weather, when full-nap fleece is too heavy, a lightweight microfleece like this made by Day One Camouflage is ideal for active hunting.

often wear a headnet when tree stand hunting. I prefer full face masks with eye holes and elastic that goes around the back of my head to hold the mask tight against my face. I've always had good luck with Scent-Lok face masks.

For active hunting on foot, I don't like cloth face masks of any kind. During a long hike, they get hot and sticky. For anyone who wears glasses, a face mask is especially problematic, because more often than not it will fog up the person's eyeglasses right when he wants to shoot. When hunting on foot, I prefer face paint. A few streaks of black, green, brown, and white are adequate to break up the revealing outline of a hunter's face and conceal him from close-range animals.

The best concealment options for hands, of course, are gloves, as described above. During cold weather, tight wool gloves are hard to beat. During warm weather, light cotton or polyester camouflage gloves are fine. In really warm weather, I sometimes shed gloves altogether and paint my hands with camo cream.

Regardless of your camo pattern, try always to hunt so that you're obscured in the shadows, and move only when animals are looking away or have their vision blocked by tree trunks, rocks, or other animals.

**Scent Control:** Possibly the concept of scent control began with baking soda and cover-up scents. For the same reason that homemakers put baking soda in refrigerators to absorb odors, hunters have long dusted their clothes and brushed their teeth with baking soda. In addition, for years hunters have doused themselves with skunk scent, fox urine, vanilla extract, and other strong scents to cover up their own odor.

These methods worked — still do — to some degree, but they are far from foolproof. Baking soda lasts only so long, and cover scents will never totally mask human odor, because big game animals have the ability to sort out odors. For example, one day as I neared my bear bait, a bear was already pawing through the pile of rotten meat. The smell of that bait pile was overwhelming. As I stood 100 yards from the bait, watching the bear, a soft breeze swirled from me toward the bear. Within seconds he jerked his head from the rotten meat, stared my way for a few seconds, and silently slinked off into the woods. How he could distinguish my odor when he had his nose buried in rotten meat is beyond me. But he did. That's why you can never count on cover scents alone.

*In dark, evergreen forests, dark forest camo patterns will hide you well. On this hunt in the spruce and fir forests of Idaho, I am wearing Mossy Oak Breakup camouflage.*

The first major improvement in scent control came in the late 1980s with the appearance of Robinson Laboratories' Scent Shield, a spray-on product that neutralizes human odor.

*Many hunters, like Larry D. Jones, prefer camouflage face cream over a cloth face mask. Larry receives congratulations from M.R. James, founder of Bowhunter magazine, for his eastern Colorado whitetail. Note the contrast in their camouflaged and uncamouflaged faces.*

Along with scent-eliminating sprays have emerged numerous unscented, scent-eliminating soaps, as well as unscented deodorants. This total array of products, if used diligently, makes a heavy assault on human odor. Some major brands are Robinson, Wildlife Research, and Hunter's Specialties.

Specialized clothing has completed the scent-control revolution. It all started with Scent-Lok and its clothing with imbedded charcoal, a material that adsorbs odor molecules. Other companies have followed suit with various styles of charcoal-based scent-control clothing, notably ScentBlocker from Robinson Outdoors, and Supprescent from W.L. Gore. More recently, various forms of anti-microbial clothing have hit the market. V.S.I. Contain clothing has a built-in anti-microbial deodorant, and Arctic Shield weaves silver, a material with anti-microbial qualities, into its fabrics. Ab-Scent and No Trace are other brands designed to control human scent.

For maximum effect, wear both under and outer scent-control garments. For example, start with Scent-Lok BaseSlayers or Arctic Shield's X Scent Base Layer T and Pull On Pants. Then over these add any of the charcoal-based jackets and pants. And never overlook the peripherals. Add scent-control gloves to contain odor from your hands. And because breath odor can be your biggest enemy, top off your outfit with a scent-containing face mask.

In theory, all of these products work, and in practice they do also — if used properly. Here's how to use them: Take a shower with unscented soap before each hunt, apply scent-eliminating deodorant, and brush your teeth with baking soda. Spray all of your equipment — bow, pack, tree stand — and exterior clothing with scent-eliminating spray and hang the clothes outside where they can air thoroughly, or store them in a scent-proof bag where they cannot pick up foreign odors. Before walking to your stand, don your charcoal or anti-microbial clothing, and spray your boots with scent-eliminating spray. When you get into your stand and are set to hunt, pull on your scent-containing gloves and face mask. It should go without saying that wearing any exterior clothing, like a sweaty hat, will negate all of your de-scenting efforts.

*Comfort:* The range of clothing and conditions are so great that I cannot prescribe a clothing system for all bowhunting situations. Rather, I'll outline systems for two common scenarios.

## Tree Stands and Clothing

If you're hunting from a cabin on your lease in Alabama, soft cotton pants and shirt, backed up by synthetic longjohns and reliable raingear, will cover most conditions you'll face. If you get soaked or cold, you can always return to the cabin to warm up and change clothes.

But not all situations are that simple. When tree stand hunting in the Midwest or North, you'll have to give clothing more thought. Start with longjohns made of wool, or synthetic materials like Thermax, Thermastat, Polartec, or Polypropylene. For cold, windy weather, I particularly like a union suit, which eliminates any gaps between pants and shirt.

Over these, add a shirt and pants made of short-napped fleece topped off with cotton or wool gloves and a baseball cap. In mild weather, this might be all you'll need, but as the weather cools, you'll want to go to insulated pants and jacket. Three-in-one jackets are versatile under changing conditions. You can zip the liner in and out as needed to meet varying conditions.

In the Midwest, stick-tights, beggar's lice, cockleburrs, and other nasty beggars can cling to your clothes like bull terriers. I have learned through painful experience that wool, fleece, and knits are terrible in the Midwest and South. In weed-infested areas, clothing with a tightly knit exterior like Cabela's Microtex are better. Even better in really bad vegetation are flocked materials like Saddle Cloth, which have a slick, smooth surface that will not hold sticky seeds.

The head and neck are major sources of heat loss, so protecting these areas is vital for warmth. When temperatures drop, or the wind picks up to increase wind chill, add a knit sock hat. For further neck and head protection, pull on a knit or fleece face mask, and wrap a wool scarf around your neck.

In mild weather, cotton gloves are needed mostly for camouflage. When temperatures drop into the 40s and below, wool gloves will be welcome. My favorites are army surplus green wool glove liners. Most military surplus stores carry these. They're soft, quiet, and warm, and because they fit your hands snugly like a, well, like a glove, you lose little dexterity. When the temperature drops below the 30s, add mittens over your glove liners and simply pull your gloved hands from the mittens to shoot. For even greater hand warmth, use a hand muff, which is basically an insulated tube tied around your waist into which you can insert both hands. To increase warmth further, drop a couple of chemical handwarmers into the muff.

Standard footgear for tree stand hunters is knee-high rubber boots. As long as you don't work up a sweat by walking too far, they will keep your feet dry and comfortable, but most hunters wear them as much for scent control as for comfort. If you keep them free of foreign and human smells, you can walk to your stand without laying down a deer-spooking scent trail. In mild weather I prefer uninsulated models like LaCrosse Grangers. If you want to spend more money, you won't regret buying leather-lined LeChameau boots. When the weather dips into the 40s and lower, you simply switch to insulated rubber boots like LaCrosse Burleys or Cabela's Marsh boots. With the introduction of scent-reduction products such as Supprescent into boots, many hunters have traded their rubber boots for standard hiking boots with scent-elimination liners. These come in insulation levels from zero up to 1,000-gram Thinsulate insulation to match the conditions. When the weather hits the 20s or lower, pac boots with felt liners, or rubber "moon" boots insulated with a layer of trapped air, will keep your feet warm.

On a recent hunting trip near Edmonton, Alberta, I wore military "moon" boots, and found they kept my feet fairly comfortable during several hours in a tree stand at temperatures down to about 10 degrees. To enhance the warmth, I placed chemical handwarmers on my toes. And on the coldest days I added Ice Breaker insulated overboots.

## Tree Stand and Gear

If I must hike a long way to my hunting area, I use a daypack with a plastic frame and strap my stand and steps to the pack. If I'm hunting a place that requires little walking, I attach shoulder straps to the stand platform and use it as my pack (many stands come equipped with shoulder straps) and hang my tree stand pack full of gear on the stand.

For tree stand hunting, a small fanny pack or rucksack will probably be adequate. In my opinion, the main criteria for a tree stand pack are quiet, quiet, and quiet. For this reason, I like an unlined pack made of synthetic fleece or wool so I can reach in and extract items silently. A nylon lining makes a pack more durable and weather resistant, but it also makes it noisier. Personally I'd rather take my chances with the quiet pack, and if rain starts falling I cover the pack with a waterproof cover. A pack with several compartments can increase organization and convenience, and a loop at the top for hanging the pack on a hook is always handy. I like to hang my pack by a loop at the top and then snap the waist belt around the tree to form a stable organizer for my tree stand.

**Following is a list of gear I would carry during an average day of tree stand hunting:**

| | |
|---|---|
| Fixed-position stand and climbing ladders; | Hand muff and chemical handwarmers |
| Or climbing stand | Scent elimination spray |
| Climbing belt | Attractor scents |
| Safety harness | Rubber gloves |
| Rattling horns | Compass |
| Grunt call | Flashlight |
| Bleat call | Relief bottle |
| Florian Ratchet Cut pruning shears | Lunch |
| Saw | Knife |
| Two pull-up ropes | Notebook |
| Reflective trail markers | Camera |
| Hangers for bow and other gear | Water |
| | Rangefinder |

*For comfort in hunting from a tree stand, dress in layers so you can shed or add clothing as needed for comfort during changing conditions.*

# Mountain/Northern Hunting

If you're hunting elk in the Rocky Mountains or caribou in Alaska, clothing selection may affect not only your comfort and hunting ability but your survival. The emphasis must be on flexibility, silence, and breathability. The same heavily insulated pants and coats that might be ideal for cold-weather tree stand hunting will be worthless for active mountain hunting.

For mule deer and antelope during August in the western states, soft, lightweight, cotton clothing, a baseball-style cap, and lightweight canvas shoes or uninsulated boots may be adequate. Add a lightweight, packable raingear for the occasional rainstorm, and summer-weight longjohns and a light jacket for chilly mornings, and you just about have it.

But in the mountains, you're wise to leave all cotton clothing at home, including cotton T-shirts and underwear. That's because cotton absorbs and retains moisture and dries very slowly. Thus, if you get damp from sweat or precipitation — both likely events in mountain and northern hunting — you could stay damp for hours and turn into a case of hypothermia just waiting to happen. Reserve clothing containing cotton, including flannel and denim, for wearing in the car and around camp. For backcountry hunting, you have far better choices.

Lightweight synthetic materials made of polyester are best: Polartec, Thermax, Cabela's Microtex and MTP, and a host of materials broadly called microfleece are excellent for active, backcountry hunting, because they are quiet, they insulate fairly well when damp, and they dry quickly. Acrylic and wool, and blends of polyester, acrylic, and wool are also good choices for outer clothing on backcountry hunts.

While I've listed the above in light weights for mild weather, all of these come in various weights up to and including heavy, full-napped fleeces like the original Arctic Fleece and

*The LaCrosse Burley has probably been the No. 1 rubber boot used by bowhunters. LaCrosse has recently updated this popular boot, making it warmer and more comfortable. This new version has a lug, self-cleaning sole.*

PolarFleece, and from very light wool to cast-iron brands like Sleeping Indian, Woolrich, King of the Mountain, and Filson. For hunting from late September on in the mountains, and for most hunting in Alaska and northern Canada, heavy outerwear should be a staple of your clothing system.

You'll also find any number of parkas and pants insulated with Thinsulate insulation and similar synthetic materials, and waterproofed with Gore-Tex, Dry Plus or other waterproof/breathable layers, and often with Scent-Lok technology, and these are more than welcome in cold, backcountry conditions.

However, I consider insulated garments far better for sedentary hunting. For hunting animals like elk and moose, where you're constantly hiking and pursuing, multiple layers of uninsulated garments are better, in my opinion. Uninsulated garments are more flexible, allowing you to move more quickly and quietly, and they're more versatile in that you can shed or add light layers to match your activity level and regulate your body heat.

To your outer layers add appropriate undergarments. As in outer layers, consider wearing only synthetic materials. Some of the more popular are Thermastat, Thermax, and polypropylene. These all come in several weights — polar or military, heavy, medium, and light or silk weights. The military and heavy weights generally are too hot for active hunting and are better reserved for stand hunting. For hunting on the move, medium and light weights are far better and more versatile. Silk is another popular, comfortable material that gives welcome warmth on chilly mornings.

To top off your clothing system add quality raingear. For backcountry hunting, you can break raingear down into two styles: 1) Packable emergency raingear, like Cabela's Rain-Lite Rainwear, made of lightweight nylon can be rolled up and stuffed into a fanny pack. This is the one place where I would make an exception and let nylon into my wardrobe. But here I consider it more of an emergency garment for sudden rainstorms in normally dry

*When temperatures start to drop, you must protect your head and neck, the areas of major heat loss. Wear a full face mask, sock hat, and scarf. On your hands, wear mittens or a full hand muff, like this model from Ice Breaker.*

country. You normally would not hunt in this raingear but just slip it on to sit out a sudden rainstorm and then continue hunting. 2) Light, uninsulated styles waterproofed with a soft, quiet outer shell coated with breathable materials like Gore-Tex and Dry Plus are best for active hunting. These models of raingear are ideal in fairly wet conditions where you actually will hunt in your raingear.

To this you would add a light crusher or baseball cap, plus a knit sock hat or similar warm hat for cold spells. My favorite gloves for active hunting are wool military glove liners. Fitting your hands snugly, they don't hamper dexterity, they'll keep your hands warm when wet, and they're cheap — about $4 at any military surplus store. Alternate three or four pairs, and you'll always have dry gloves ready to go. For cold spells and working around camp, add waterproof insulated gloves or mittens.

For distance hiking, the lighter your footwear, the better. An old adage says that one pound on the feet equals five pounds on the back. I'm not sure how anyone could measure that precisely, but I do know that when wearing lighter shoes I can hike longer and with less fatigue than when wearing heavy boots.

My favorite shoes for elk hunting are Cabela's Silent Stalk canvas hunting shoes. They're similar to the old Converse tennis shoes except that they're camouflaged and contain Supprescent. For wet days I wear Gore-Tex socks in my canvas shoes and have found this combination pretty reliable for keeping my feet dry. When constant rain threatens, or the terrain is wet and boggy as it often is on the northern tundra, I wear Cabela's Gore-Tex Supprescent Silent Stalk Sneaker boots. They are light in weight, but they're also rugged and waterproof. For general mountain and northern hunting, I see

*The lighter your footwear, the farther you can hike without fatigue. Some of my favorite footwear for backcountry hunting is Cabela's Silent Stalk Sneakers, which are feather light.*

no reason for heavy hiking boots.

Lightweight footwear is not ideal for all conditions. If you're goat or sheep hunting on steep shale slopes, or you're backpacking heavy loads, you'll want heavy boots with good ankle support, heavy soles to protect the bottoms of your feet from rock bruises, and lug or air-bob soles for traction. Danner, Meindl, Rocky, Browning, and others make good heavy-duty hiking boots.

To finish off foot comfort, pick the right socks. The general advice is to wear lightweight, synthetic liner socks against your feet to wick moisture away from your feet and wool socks over these to cushion the feet and absorb moisture. Theoretically, slippage takes place between the two pairs of socks, rather than against your feet to prevent blisters.

In the northern states and across Canada and Alaska, you can count on bugs — mosquitoes, black flies, no-see-ums — during any warm weather. They're especially bad during spring bear seasons and caribou hunts in August and early September. An absolute must during these times is net clothing. One brand I've used is the Bug Tamer. In really warm weather, I wear only the mesh pants and jacket over light underwear and T-shirt. In cooler weather, a headnet added over regular hunting clothes is adequate. In cases where bugs are severe and you must expose skin in order to shoot, protect exposed skin with a Deet-based insect repellent.

Now, let's summarize: If you're driving to a camp, you can throw in all the clothes you own, so you might not have to give your selection a lot of thought. But if you're backpacking, packing in on horses, or flying in on a Super Cub, you'll have to be more selective. I suggest you pack two outer garments: one microfleece, one heavy fleece or wool; two sets of longjohns, light and medium weight; raingear; lightweight hiking shoes and waterproof boots; wool gloves and mittens; two or three pairs of socks; and a bug suit.

In wet climates and for floating rivers, pack your gear in waterproof boat bags. Rather than packing all your gear in one or two big bags, pack it in several smaller bags. That is especially valuable when you're flying on a bush plane, because it's far easier for the pilot to pack several small bags than one big one.

# Backcountry Hunting Pack

Hunting packs will vary greatly, depending on where and how you're hunting. A pack for hunting elk, mule deer, or other western game generally must be roomy, because you have to include survival gear and other items needed in the backcountry. In the West or Far North, a hunting pack is critical for two reasons: 1) You never know when you're going to get caught out, far from camp, in life-threatening weather. Your pack, always equipped with survival gear, could save your life. 2) The best times to hunt are at daybreak and at dusk. If you're worried about getting back to camp by dark, you'll lose many opportunities to take elk or other wilderness game. With a pack equipped not only with survival gear but with gear for navigating in the dark, you simply will hunt longer and better. For these reasons, I attribute much of my backcountry success to my hunting pack.

Some off-road hunters use large fanny packs, but more popular these days are double-decker fanny packs with shoulder straps that help support some of the weight, and rucksacks with waist belts to support the weight.

I personally carry these concepts a step further by using a hunting pack with a small plastic frame. The frame, equipped with a mesh back band and padded hip belt, holds the pack away from my back to reduce sweating, and it supports the pack so I can carry 10 to 15 pounds of

**Following is a standard list of gear I carry in my pack for off-road hunting:**

| | | |
|---|---|---|
| Map | Moleskin | Sweater |
| Compass | Soap | Raingear |
| GPS | Neosporin | Waterproof pack cover |
| Flashlight with extra | 50-foot nylon cord | Bow repair items |
| batteries and bulb | Signal whistle | Bowstring |
| Lighter and waterproof | Signal mirror | Axle keepers |
| matches | Plastic tape | Arrow rest |
| Firestarters | Water filter | Allen wrench |
| Hunting knife | Water | Camera and film |
| Sharpening steel | Notebook | Hunting license and tags |
| Folding saw | Pen | Game bags |
| First-aid kit | Predator call | |
| Band-Aids | Wind checker | Plus, if conditions dictate: |
| Gauze pads | Pack cover | Insect repellent |
| Adhesive tape | Toilet paper | Snakebite kit |
| Gauze roll | Needle and thread | Sunscreen |
| Aspirin | Food | Sunglasses |

hunting gear with no strain on my shoulders. The compact pack and frame does not obstruct my shooting, and it has a quiet, fleece outer surface, so I can slip through the brush with scarcely a whisper. If your pack is so heavy, bulky, or obtrusive that you feel compelled to take it off to shoot — or you're tempted to leave it in camp on occasion — you need a new pack. A more comfortable pack. A lighter pack.

## Final Thoughts

A discussion on equipment could continue endlessly, so let's summarize it in one statement — prepare for all contingencies. If you're hunting off-road, always include survival gear: fire-starting materials; navigation tools (compass, GPS, map); lightweight shelter (space blanket, plastic for making quick shelter); folding saw or multi-tool (for making fires, shelters); high-energy bars; first-aid kit. For tree stand hunting, a cell phone can be a lifesaver — assuming you're hunting in an area with cellular access. In remote Alaska, a satellite phone can be worth the expense and weight. On any remote hunt, signal flares could save your life.

And always give camp gear full attention. Obviously, if you're hunting from your home, from a lodge, out of a motel, or out of a camp trailer or truck camper, you're pretty well assured of a dry, secure camp. But what if you're hunting off-road on a fly-in hunt, float trip, backpacking adventure, or horse packing trip? In these cases, you are at the mercy of the weather.

Above all, equip yourself with a high-quality tent and sleeping bag. On a hunt in Alaska, my friend Gary Christoffersen and I got hit with an unseasonable blizzard. We had a good dome tent, but the furious wind and drifting snow broke several of the poles, collapsing the tent. For a while, we thought we might die out there on the tundra, and only our first-rate sleeping bags kept us warm as we huddled for several hours in our flattened tent under a rising snowdrift. Fortunately, the storm mercifully ended before we smothered to death, but you can bet we learned the value of a good tent.

In the high mountains and Far North, you can never predict weather, so you simply must prepare for the worst. You'll never regret going prepared.

*In the high country, a quality tent like this is essential equipment. It not only assures pleasant camping but could save your life.*

In truly remote country of the Far North, where you're isolated from all help, a satellite phone is a link to civilization that could save lives. Here, Alaskan outfitter Preston Cavner used his satellite phone to check on news from the outside world.

*Chapter 7*

# Stand Hunting

**B**ack in my early days of bowhunting — in the dark ages before videos, countless books on bowhunting, widespread seminars, and all the other information sources we enjoy today — my friends and I essentially rambled through the woods and fields, hoping to get "some shooting." Occasionally we winged arrows at deer bounding off through the trees or sage, but our approach could best be described as random. We had no plan and enjoyed very little success.

Our approach was a carryover from rifle hunting. Many rifle hunters call this still-hunting, but in fact they simply walk through the woods, and when they jump a deer, they blaze away. It's a careless approach, but it often works, because a rifle can compensate for a lot of hunting errors.

A bow, on the other hand, cannot. If you make a mistake in technique or performance, you'll see nothing but white tails waving through the trees, leaving you frustrated and hopeless. The bow and arrow offers little leeway. The only acceptable shot

*In some situations, permanent stands make sense. If you own or lease your own land, and hunt the same locations year after year, a well-built stand will serve you well. Cecil Carder is hunting from a stand built into a live oak in Texas.*

*Tree stands offer multiple advantages for bowhunters. It's small wonder that 80 percent of all whitetail deer taken by bowhunters are taken by archers in tree stands. I killed this buck from a tree stand in Illinois.*

is a broadside shot at a calm, stationary animal. To get that kind of shot, random roaming and hoping are not good enough. You must have a plan. That's what we discuss here — the plans best suited to getting you the requisite broadside shots at close-range big game.

## Reasons for Tree Stands

Prior to 1970, tree stands not only were scarce, they actually were illegal in some states. But with the commercial development of climbing stands and easy-to-use hang-on stands, along with legalization of tree stands in all states, the popularity of hunting with tree stands exploded in the 1970s. Today, many hunters would not think of hunting whitetail deer — and many other species of game — without tree stands. In my opinion, tree stands have contributed more to the rising success of bowhunters than any other single item, including the compound bow.

That's because you can summarize the essence of bowhunting success in one sentence: *You must see game animals before they see you.* Regardless of hunting method, if you can see animals before they see you, you've won 90 percent of the battle. That's why visibility is the major advantage of hunting from a tree. Unless you're performing rap on your stand platform, you will virtually always see approaching animals before they see you. At that point, you are in control.

You gain this "see 'em first" advantage primarily because of your lofty position. If you're sitting on the ground, you may see into the brush 20 or 30 feet. From a tree stand in that same location, you might see 100 feet or farther, and by looking down onto the cover, you can detect slight movements you would never see by looking through cover from ground level.

Just as significant, most animals don't look for danger in trees. It is true that in regions where bow season runs for months, deer do learn to scan the trees for danger. In Alabama I was perched in a big oak tree at the edge of a field late one January evening when two does approached. Seeing them first, I froze against the trunk of the tree, waiting for them to walk past to offer me a shot. But even as I sat motionless, one of the does glanced up, apparently saw me silhouetted against the sky, and, of course, started blowing, which alerted every other deer nearby.

Nevertheless, you're far more likely to remain undetected in a tree than on the ground. One morning in northern Idaho I had just finished rattling antlers when I saw a six-point whitetail heading my way. That deer spent 10 minutes directly under my stand, looking for the source of that rattling, but not once did he look up at me, 12 feet straight overhead. That's fairly typical.

Finally, your high position lets you get away with movement you never would on the ground. In most cases you can turn on your stand platform and draw to shoot without being seen, whereas on the ground you have to time such movements perfectly.

Given all of the above, you can see why you'll probably get 10 shots at close-range game while hunting from a tree stand for every one you would get on the ground. No wonder 80 percent of all whitetail deer taken by bowhunters are taken by tree stand hunters.

## Kinds of Stands

Essentially you have five options — climbing, hang-on, ladder, permanent, and tripod — and your choice depends largely on your approach to hunting and the kinds of trees in your area.

Climbing stands generally come in two sections — foot platform and seat/climbing aid. To climb with the stand you attach both sections to the tree with a steel bar, chain, or cable, depending on brand, and then climb by alternately raising the seat section and the foot platform. Climbers are great for mobile hunting, because you can be 15 feet off the ground, ready to hunt, within 10 minutes or so, and, overall, they're relatively light. The stands themselves weigh more than hang-on stands of comparable size, but you don't need climbing steps, so the overall climbing system weighs about the same. Most climbers weigh between 10 and 20 pounds. On the downside, some climbers can be a bit noisy as you attach them to a tree and climb with them. And the trees in your area must be fairly straight and limbless.

Despite their limitations, climbing stands are ideal in some areas. Hunting whitetails in the Pacific Northwest, I commonly roam about with a lightweight climber on my back. Anyplace I find fresh sign I make a quick setup. The lodgepole pine and fir trees there have straight trunks with few limbs. I only have to snip off a few small branches as I climb to reach my hunting position. In the South, bowhunters prowl the woods, looking for oak trees dropping acorns. When they find such a treasure, they immediately climb a nearby tree with a straight limbless trunk and wait for deer to visit the banquet table.

Hang-on stands are excellent for mobile hunting. These platforms, most of which have built-in seats, attach to trees with a chain or strap. You need a climbing system to ascend the tree to install the stand. The most common climbing systems are screw-in or strap-on steps; climbing sticks with a central column and steps welded or bolted to it; sectioned ladders; and lineman's climbing spikes. Hang-ons can be a little more difficult to put up than climbers, and installing steps and stand can be dangerous unless you use the proper safety gear.

On the plus side, hang-ons are relatively compact and light in weight. Small hang-ons weigh from 6 to 10 pounds. When you add climbing gear the whole setup weighs between 10 and 20 pounds. Hang-ons are fairly quick to use — with practice you can be in place within 20 minutes — and you can put hang-ons in trees with plenty of limbs.

You can leave a hang-on in hunting position for a day or two, allowing you to quickly climb in for a second or third hunt, a convenience not available with a climber. One of my favorite approaches is to put up a hang-on for an afternoon hunt, leave it in place when I quit at dark, and to hunt from it again the next morning. For that second sit, I can silently climb into my stand in seconds. After that, I generally move to a new location.

If you hunt the same lands day after day, you might install hang-on stands for the season. When mobility is not an issue, larger, heavier hang-ons with bigger platforms give you welcome additional foot room and comfort. If stand theft is a concern, you can remove the bottom treesteps. That won't stop determined thieves, but it will remove temptation for honest people. You can also padlock a chain around the stand to deter theft.

Ladder stands are a good alternative to hang-on stands. This is a generic term for stands that consist of a ladder with a built-in platform at the top. The strong points for ladder stands are stability and ease in climbing. For beginning bowhunters who have no experience with treesteps, for young hunters just getting started in tree stand hunting, and for older folks who might feel a little shaky on treesteps, ladder stands are perfect. Many outfitters, who get a mix of clients with varied climbing abilities, rely heavily on ladders.

Ladders do have their limitations: Compared to climbers and hang-ons, they are relatively heavy and bulky. Thus, they are not readily portable. While one person can put up most ladder stands, the process is a lot easier with two people. For these reasons, most hunters use ladder stands as semipermanent stands.

Permanent stands are good if you own your own land and have some carpentry skills, because over a period of years permanent stands will save you time and effort. But they have their shortcomings. While the bother of building permanent stands would be an obstacle for a lot of us, the real problem with permanent stands is deterioration. The lumber can weaken over time, and the expanding trunks and limbs of growing trees can pull nails loose. Unless you're fully committed to a piece of property and to maintaining your stands, you're better off buying high-quality commercial stands, putting them up before the season, and taking them down afterwards.

Tripod stands (and quadpods) are essentially tripods 10 to 12 feet high with a rotating seat on top. These gained popularity in the brush

*Climbing stands allow you to move rapidly from one position to another, and they're self-contained, and require no steps or ladders. Used correctly, they are very safe stands. In this photo, Brand Ferris is using an Ol' Man climber.*

country of Texas where no trees grow large enough to hold stands. Placed in front of heavy cover so the hunter is not silhouetted, tripods are remarkably effective.

On one hunt in Texas, I set up a ground blind near a feeder, and well hidden, I was sure the deer would not see me. Mistake! Every deer that came to that feeder detected me and refused to come within range. So the next night the landowner and I set up a tripod stand. Even though I was not nearly as well concealed on the tripod, which sat only 15 yards from the feeder, several deer came in without hesitation, as if I did not exist. Tripods have broad application in any good game country lacking big trees. On a brown bear hunt in Alaska, my friends and I placed tripods in the willows along a salmon stream, and they worked just as well there as they do in Texas.

*Portable hang-on stands are probably the most widely used among bowhunters. They're light, easy to put up, and stable. They can be left in place to function as permanent stands. Jay McAninch is hunting in Iowa.*

Tripods are easy and safe to use, especially for people who feel uncomfortable climbing trees. On the downside, they're heavy and bulky, so they're hardly ideal for mobile hunting.

## Trees and Safety

Without question, climbing trees is the most dangerous part of bowhunting. The National Bowhunter Education Foundation (NBEF) estimates that one out of three bowhunters will suffer a fall at least once during their hunting lives. While lucky hunters get away with minor accidents like broken arms or legs, the less fortunate end up as paraplegics or quadriplegics, and many die. Make no mistake — falling from tree stands is common, and it is deadly.

Yet virtually all tree stand accidents are preventable. Some occur because of equipment failure, so before every use, check your stand and steps for weak, broken, or worn parts. Far more occur because of brain failure. People climb trees as if they are exempt from falling. That means 1) they take chances in how and where they climb and 2) they wear no safety equipment to prevent falls or to catch themselves if they do fall.

A tree stand hunter's most valuable equipment item is his safety harness. Yet, amazingly, some people still refuse to wear a safety harness, and a person can only conclude that they're suicidal. Perched high on a stand platform, you can easily lose your balance, make a wrong step (especially under the influence of buck fever), or fall asleep and tumble to the ground.

The NBEF strongly urges the use of a full-body harness rather than a safety belt around the waist. Harnesses not only have straps around the chest but also around the legs. And the tether that connects you to the tree is placed at the top of the harness. Thus, if you fall, the leg straps will support part of your weight, and the tether will hold you upright. In contrast, a single strap could tighten around your waist or chest and suffocate you, and it also could allow you to hang helplessly upside down, which could be as bad as or worse than falling to the ground.

Here's one other thought about use of a harness: When you're on stand, eliminate slack from the tether. You should be able to lean out against the tether without falling off your stand. That way the harness won't just catch you if you fall; it will prevent your falling. That, in my opinion, is the real purpose for a safety belt or harness — preventing falls.

The most dangerous moments in tree stand hunting are when you're climbing into or out of your stand. Surveys show that a high percentage of tree stand accidents occur at these critical times. How do you protect yourself at these vulnerable moments? Use a climbing belt in conjunction with your safety harness. Good harnesses have D rings on the waist strap for attachment of a climbing belt. Always use the climbing belt as you install treesteps and hang your stand — not only to prevent your falling, but to free your hands for work.

Once you have your stand installed, and before you climb onto the platform, attach the tether of your safety harness above the stand. Now release your climbing belt and step onto the platform. You're never without fall protection. When you start to get down, do the reverse. Before unhooking the tether, step off the platform onto the top step. Hook your climbing belt around the tree below the stand, and then unhook the safety tether. Again, you're protected at all times.

Finally, on the subject of safety, never try to hand-carry gear into the stand. Equip your stands with pull-up cords. Before ascending your tree, attach your bow and other gear to the cord, and when you're firmly harnessed into your stand, pull the gear up to you.

## Trees and Wisdom

The first criterion for any stand location is the presence of animals, of course, but you first must consider huntability. If you telegraph your presence to the deer you're hunting, you'll see few animals — and get good shots at fewer still.

*Tripod or quadpod stands are widely used in brush country lacking trees large enough to hold tree stands. They gained popularity in the brush country of South Texas, but they adapt well to any brush country. These brown bear hunters are sitting in quadpods set in willows on the shore of a lake in Alaska.*

Above all, you must understand the nature of the wind in your area and always place your stands downwind of the trail, sign, water, or food source you're hunting. If the wind is variable in your area, prepare two stand sites. For example, if you're hunting a trail, put stands on both the east and west sides of the trail. Then if the wind switches, you can quickly change locations to keep the wind in your favor.

In some locations, this is not possible. If that's the case in any prime spot, simply stay out of there until the wind is right. Experienced hunters will wait for days to hunt certain locations until the wind is just right. You never want to take the chance on fouling up a prime location by hunting it when deer have any possibility of smelling you.

Try to situate all stands so you can get into and out of them without disturbing any animals. To reach one of my favorite stands in Iowa, I waded 200 yards down a creek and then climbed a steep bank to pop directly into my stand. This approach allowed me to reach the stand without passing through any deer cover. Wherever possible, approach from a waterway, open field, road, path, a yard, or any sterile area where you won't disturb or alert the deer you're hunting.

Similarly, always approach from downwind. Big game animals don't have to see or hear you to know you're there. If they catch the faintest whiff of you en route to your stand, you probably will never see them. They may not move out of the area, but they will avoid the area around your stand. Put just as much thought into your approach route as you do into the deers' approach route.

While deer may not regularly inspect the treetops for danger, they'll definitely spot you up there if you're obvious. If at all possible, place your stands in trees where you're surrounded by concealing foliage. That's easy enough early in the season before hardwoods lose their leaves. And evergreens always provide good cover. On any tree, cut out only as many branches as necessary to get clear shots.

In the absence of foliage — commonly the case late in the season — try to put your stands in trees with trunks wide enough to eliminate your silhouette. And when trees are naked, try to set up with trees or hills behind you, so you are not silhouetted against the sky.

How high should you climb? Some hunters say 10 to 12 feet is more than high enough, while others swear that anything less than 30 feet is too low. Obviously, the higher you climb, the less likely deer are to see or smell you.

High stands create problems. Some people get squeamish

*The most valuable equipment for tree stand hunting is a safety harness such as the full-body harness in use above. When on stand, adjust the tether on your safety harness to eliminate all slack. That way the harness doesn't just stop you if you fall; it prevents your falling.*

*Always use a climbing belt to climb up to the stand, and then attach your safety harness before unhooking the climbing belt.*

when they climb too high — only you can decide that for yourself. My comfort limit is about 20 feet. And ultrahigh stands create poor shot angles. If you're 30 feet high and a deer stands 10 yards from your tree, you're basically shooting straight down on his back, which is a poor shot.

On the other hand, unless you have good cover, you will probably be spotted regularly in stands 10 to 12 feet off the ground. Obviously, lots of variables govern stand height. However, as a general rule, I have found 15 to 20 feet about right in most situations. Below 15 feet, you can scarcely breathe or move without being seen, and above 20 feet, you often have so much foliage between you and the deer, and the shooting angle is so steep, you might not get quality broad-side shots. In regard to concealment, I have rarely felt the need to be higher than 20 feet. When putting up stands, I like to tie an 18-foot pull-up cord to my belt. Then, as I climb and the cord begins to tighten, I know my exact height. It's just a simple gauge to indicate the desired height.

If you're hunting hit and run, you won't want to spend a lot of time clearing major shooting lanes. That will create a lot of noise at critical times and spread human scent around your stand area. If you're using a fixed-position stand, put your stand up and then look around from your stand to identify the best potential shooting lanes. With these in mind, climb down and cut away troublesome twigs and branches. Avoid handling limbs with your bare hands. Either wear rubber gloves or reach up with your cutting tool and cut the branches without touching them.

If you're using a climbing stand, you won't want to go up and down the tree to check shooting lanes. So, before climbing up, walk around your stand tree and visualize shooting lanes from the ground. Then clear them out before you climb the tree.

Once settled into your stand, cut out any limbs that might restrict your shooting. Always draw your bow a few times to make sure you can draw and aim unobstructed. Cut out any branches that could possibly get in your way. If you hunt the same land regularly, cut shooting lanes well ahead of time. In the spring or summer, identify good stand trees and clear ample shooting lanes. Use a pole saw or pruner to cut out-of-reach limbs. Do a good job of clearing now, and you can hunt without distractions or further disturbance come fall.

In a situation like this, you have several options: You can place a stand in every one of your cleared locations; you can simply clear around potential stand trees and then put up your stand at the time you hunt; or you can place stand brackets or screw-in mounting pins in these trees and then climb up and hang your stand whenever you hunt that location. Using systems like these, you can hunt many positions with only one platform. Some Canadian whitetail outfitters place stand brackets in dozens of trees, and when they want a client to hunt a specific spot, they simply give him a stand platform, which he hangs on the bracket. It's a quick, quiet method that keeps cost down and prevents other hunters from stealing or hunting from the outfitter's stands.

## Stand Location for Whitetails

Because of their nature, habits, and habitat, whitetails are the big game most perfectly suited to tree stand hunting. Data from the Pope & Young Club records show that bowhunters take rough-ly 80 percent of their whitetail deer by hunting from tree stands, and the only other animals that come close to that level are bears, and that's only because many bears are taken over bait.

In a broad sense, you look for two kinds of locations to ambush whitetails — travel routes and destinations. Let's look at each:

**Travel Routes:** Early in the fall, prior to the rut, and then again late in the season after the rut, you commonly will ambush whitetails traveling between bedding and feeding areas, to and from water, or away from disturbance. During the rut, bucks might not be traveling between specific destinations but may simply be traveling far and wide, looking for does or checking sign. Regardless of time of year or the purpose of their movements, whitetails tend to follow fairly predictable travel routes. Your challenge is to identify those routes and to place stands there to intercept the deer.

**Funnels:** As a general rule, whitetails will stick to any available cover to hide their movements. The trick is to find a place where the cover narrows down enough to guarantee that any deer traveling through that cover will come within bow range of your stand. That narrow spot would be called a funnel.

Farmland and prairies present the most obvious funnels. Any narrow strip of trees or brush connecting two larger blocks of woods is an obvious funnel. In the prairie states, narrow cottonwood bottoms form clearcut funnels. Hunting in grasslands of South Dakota, a friend and I saw a buck enter a narrow strip of cottonwoods along a river bottom. We drove around to the far end, where I waited for the buck. Not long afterward he predictably came snooping up through the cover of the bottom, and I greeted him with an arrow.

The situation was similar in western Kansas. My friend Gary Nichols and I were concerned about finding a place where we could put a stand, because 99 percent of the country was open grasslands. Finally, in a narrow strip of cottonwoods in a dry wash, we found enough fresh tracks and scrapes to tell us deer were regularly traveling that wash. So I put a stand in one of the scant cottonwoods.

*Always place stands so you can get into them without disturbing the deer you're hunting. One of the best ways to approach a stand is by wading up a creek. In Iowa I used this shallow creek as a scent-free approach trail to my stand.*

*If possible, place your stands in trees with concealing foliage. If that is not possible, try to put them in trees with fairly large trunks that will eliminate your silhouette, as this hunter has done.*

The tree was so sparse, I gathered up a bunch of tumbleweeds and stuffed them into the branches around my stand to give me some semblance of cover. Late one afternoon, a hefty ten-pointer came sneaking through the trees in that wash, and I shot him at a distance of 17 yards.

In expansive woods, funnels are not so obvious. I've hunted whitetails many times in northwestern Montana where the forests of spruce and fir stretch for endless miles. I found a place between a couple of small marshes about 75 yards apart. The narrow strip of woods effectively formed a funnel, so I put a stand in the middle of that strip, figuring any deer traveling between those two marshes would have to pass within 25 to 30 yards of my stand. For two straight years I killed bucks in that spot. It was an effective funnel.

Barriers also create funnels. On a plantation I hunted in Alabama, some of the best stands were placed at the outside corners of creeks where the high banks and deep water prevented deer from crossing. The high banks formed effective barriers that funneled deer along predictable paths. A corollary to this is river crossings. On any deep stream or river, deer will have favorite shallow crossing points. On the Blackfoot River in Montana, a fairly deep and swift river, I found that shallow crossing points presented some of the best stand sites.

While deer can jump fences with ease, they will, in areas with high, tight fences, seek easy crossing points. Look for points where the top strand is sagging or broken, or where the fence spans a ditch to create a gap where deer can easily crawl under the fence.

In the mountains of central Idaho, barriers are more commonly cliffs or rock slides. As the deer traverse steep terrain from one mountain bench or flat ridge top to another, they often pass close to these barriers — and to my tree stands.

***Terrain:*** The first time I ever hunted in Illinois, my companion directed me to a stand on a "ridge." Analyzing the terrain carefully, I could only ask, "Ridge?" You see, I live in Idaho, and to me the term "ridge" refers to a rise in terrain of at least 2,000 vertical feet. "Where is the ridge?" I asked. "The land looks flat to me."

"Flat?" my companion said, incredulous. "Don't you see that vegetation line where those oak trees are growing? The ground is clearly higher there. The deer follow that higher ground."

The lesson then is to look for any slight change in terrain. In the Midwest or South, such terrain changes could be very subtle, like that Illinois ridge. And generally the terrain feature is a rise, or steepening of the terrain. In steep western mountains, terrain changes could be far more obvious, and they are more likely places where the topography flattens out. In particular, whitetails tend to follow benches and flatter ridge tops, making these places good bets for stands.

Generally, whitetails will follow paths of least resistance, so in any territory try to identify terrain where the deer will expend the least amount of energy to travel from one point to another. Saddles — the lowest points between drainages — are always likely places for stands. These generally are obvious in western mountains. In flatter regions, saddles are subtle, but they are usually no less appealing to traveling whitetails.

Topographic maps can be priceless in identifying terrain-dictated travel routes. Study contour lines to identify any rises in flat terrain or any points where steep terrain levels out even slightly.

***Vegetation Lines:*** It goes without saying that deer stick to cover whenever possible. But how do you distinguish travel routes where cover is continuous? That's the case in much of the Deep South, and the hunters there generally look for places where different kinds of vegetation meet — where bamboo meets hardwoods, pines meet hardwoods, willows meet pines. Wherever you hunt, vegetation lines can be good stand locations. And if you find a place where three vegetation types come together, you've found an even better place.

In parts of some prairie states, cover seems totally lacking. Don't overlook the value of weedy fence lines. In the absence of fully concealing cover, deer often will follow or bed in the slim cover provided by fencerows, swales, ditches, or canals.

## Destinations

***Food and Water Sources:*** Isolated food sources are always good places for stands. White oak trees are legendary for their deer drawing ability in late October. Hunting the Tar Hollow State Forest in Ohio, I was searching a ridge top when I jumped several deer. Investigating, I found the ground torn up under a couple of white oaks and could see some fresh acorns on the ground. Immediately, I found a good tree for my stand and climbed up. A couple of hours later I killed a fine nine-point buck coming in for a midmorning snack of acorns. Any other kind of mast-bearing trees, as well as fruit trees, always have good potential as stand locations.

Throughout whitetail range, and particularly in the Midwest, corn and soybean fields probably provide the bulk of feed for whitetails. Alfalfa and clover fields rank high as food sources in farm country. And in the South, greenfields are always a draw through the fall and winter. Taking a stand right at the edge of these fields is standard procedure for many southern hunters.

In western forests, clearcuts of five to 10 years of age produce nutritious brouse that will attract deer. Even logging operations can be deer magnets, because moss on treetop limbs is like candy to deer, and logging puts a lot of tasty moss within reach. If you can't set up directly on a food source, try to place your stand to intercept whitetails as they travel from a bedding to a feeding site.

In dry areas you can also do well by taking a stand near water. In Wisconsin, outfitter Tom Indrebo has created small, isolated water holes throughout his farmland hunting areas, and his hunters do very well from stands overlooking these water holes. The prairie states are typically dry, so stock ponds and water tanks regularly produce shots for bowhunters. In Idaho, I found an isolated spring on top of a dry ridge that was pounded with deer tracks. Setting up a stand there, I had several deer come within range and eventually killed a buck.

**Bedding Areas:** During the day, deer generally lie-up in the thickest, most impenetrable tangles of brush they can find. Many experienced whitetail hunters adamantly insist you should never hunt these places, because disturbance here could permanently push deer right out of your hunting area. Other hunters say these are the best places to kill big bucks.

If you cannot catch a buck in the open during daylight, your only option may be to hunt him in his bedroom. If you decide to do that, put your stand at the fringes of the bedding cover (always downwind), and plan your approach so you can get into and out of the stand without being seen, heard, or smelled by any deer that might be occupying the cover. You can hunt bedding areas if you do it carefully.

**Fresh Sign:** During the prerut and rut, fresh sign may be the single most important key for stand placement. In many areas throughout North America, the prerut takes place during late October and early November, and the peak of the rut falls in mid- to late November. Of course, rut timing varies by region. In parts of the South, deer may rut from October into February. So you need to understand the specifics of rut timing in your area.

During the prerut, bucks prolifically rub trees and make scrapes. Rubs and scrapes are visual and olfactory means of communication among deer. If your usual funnels and destination spots are not paying off during the prerut and rut, you might be well advised to sneak through the woods, looking for fresh rubs and scrapes. A concentration of such fresh sign could very well be the best clue for a stand site. Particularly in the big woods of the Northwest, I have had some of my best success by forgetting about funnels and feeding areas and simply hunting the hottest, freshest sign I can find.

Along a similar vein, always consider concentrations of does as positive buck sign, particularly during the peak of the rut and following the peak. This is when bucks will be cruising, looking for any does that have not been bred. Obviously, the places they will search first and regularly will be places where does are hanging out. Particularly during foul weather at the onset of winter, does will yard up around the best food sources, and bucks, still feeling the urge to rut, will not be far away.

# Calling, Scents, and Decoys

An indispensable addition to any tree stand setup is good calling. For whitetails, the most universal call is the grunt call, because bucks and does both make grunting sounds, and they make them year around. However, grunting is by far the most effective during the overall rut period in the fall. All call companies — Primos, Woods Wise, Lohman, Quaker Boy, and many others — make good grunt calls. The grunt most often is heard as a short, sharp *urp*. However, a buck following a doe will emit a staccato series of urps. And an angry buck trying to intimidate a smaller buck will produce a deep, drawn-out growl.

Some experienced hunters say you should blow your grunt call only when you see a buck in the distance that might not come within range. I disagree. In thick cover, how do you know when a buck might be passing by just out of sight? If you are not calling as he passes by, you will never

*In some situations, you can clear multiple trees and equip them with brackets. Then, when you're ready to hunt a site, you simply hang a platform on the bracket. Alberta whitetail outfitter Jeff Lander is placing a bracket in an aspen tree. Notice that he is using a climbing belt for safety.*

*In Kentucky, as throughout mid-America, whitetail country is a mix of farmland, woodlots, and strips of weeds. A bowhunter must analyze terrain, vegetation, and sign to determine which funnels deer travel from one field to the other.*

see him. But by calling blind, you might pull some of those bucks within range.

I recall one day in a stand in northern Idaho, where the evergreen trees are dense and limit visibility to less than 40 yards. So every minute or two I emitted a series of short grunts. Right after one of these series, a buck appeared suddenly. By the time I saw him, he was headed straight toward my tree and he ended up straight under me — much to his misfortune. If I had not been blowing my grunt call regularly, I probably never would have seen that buck.

Rattling is another valuable calling method. Rattling antlers simulates sparring or fighting between two bucks. It works best during the two to three weeks of the prerut. At this time, bucks are cruising and looking for hot does, and often they will readily investigate rattling.

Real antlers sound best, but synthetic antlers are nearly as good. Rattling bags are good when bucks are close, but they don't produce as much volume as antlers, and a major value of rattling is to attract bucks from long range. The best conditions for rattling are cold, clear, dead-still mornings when sound carries well. You can rattle-in bucks from as far as a half mile.

To rattle effectively, simply picture in your mind what two fighting bucks would sound like, and duplicate that sound. Rattle for a minute or so, pause for a few seconds, and rattle for another 30 seconds. Follow up with a couple of grunt calls. Then pick up your bow and get ready. Wait for 20 minutes to a half-hour. If no deer have showed up in that time, repeat the sequence. Continue to do that throughout the day.

The addition of a doe bleat call can enhance grunt calling and rattling. You may call-in deer with just the doe bleat, but if you add some rattling and grunting, it can be even more effective.

Don't give up if you don't immediately call-in deer. You may have to call for several hours — or days — to get a response. One afternoon in Wisconsin I climbed into my tree stand at 1 p.m. and rattled every half-hour for more than three hours. I was about to think it was futile when, at 4:15 p.m., a buck I estimated at 150-inch Pope & Young inches appeared, coming over a rise, 25 yards away. He walked directly to my stand tree, never turning to present a broadside shot. Then he looked up, and when our eyes met he bounded away. While I did not get that one, I have rattled-in and killed a couple of dozen bucks in just that way.

Scents can further enhance any stand setup. The general wisdom is that during the prerut a buck scent that arouses territorial instincts will be most effective. During the peak of the rut, doe-in-heat type scents may work better, because at this time bucks are seeking hot does. This is not always constant, however. Deer often investigate foreign smells out of curiosity as much as sexual response, and if you happen to get the wrong scent at the wrong time, it's not necessarily your undoing. Deer may simply come in to investigate that unusual aroma.

To maximize the range of any attractor scent, attach a drag rag saturated with scent to one of your boots as you walk to your stand. When you get within 20 yards or so of your stand, take the rag off your boot and hang it in a shooting lane where you want a buck to stop. For greater pulling power, tape a clothespin to an empty plastic film canister, and place a scent saturated cotton ball in the canister. At your stand, remove the cap and clip the canister to a branch.

For even more efficiency, use commercial scent dispensers. Charge these with doe-in-heat scent and hang them in your shooting lanes.

In open woods or fields where deer can see long distances, a decoy may be the final inducement needed to pull a buck within range. A buck might be passing by well out of range, but if he sees a decoy 100 yards away, he might come to investigate. A decoy works particularly well

*My tumbleweed stand in Kansas worked, as evidenced by this fine buck. While traveling a cottonwood bottom in search of does, he passed 17 yards from my tree stand.*

*In the steep terrain of western mountains, flat benches often form effective funnels. I placed my stand on a bench in the mountains of northern Idaho to take this buck.*

in conjunction with calling. If you rattle and an approaching buck cannot see a deer at the source of the rattling, he might hang up and stay well out of range. But if he sees a deer (decoy), he will have reason to investigate.

Full-bodied decoys are ideal, because they're realistic and deer can see them from all directions. However, if you're hiking a long way to your hunting area, you might prefer a lightweight silhouette.

As you carry and place a decoy, always wear rubber gloves to keep the decoy free of human scent. Place a doe decoy with its head toward brush or a tree trunk so a buck must approach from behind. Place a buck decoy just the opposite, because bucks will approach other bucks head on.

## Ground Blinds

For good reasons, tree stands are the first option for bowhunters. However, some great ambush locations have no trees, or they have no trees big enough to hold tree stands. And some people with injuries or fear of heights simply can't or won't climb trees.

Well-placed ground blinds, however, can be nearly as effective as tree stands. All of the principles discussed for tree stands — wind direction; scent control;

stand locations; use of calls, scents, and decoys — apply to ground blinds. But since a ground blind is at eye level with animals, you must take precautions you might not take with a tree stand.

The simplest ground blind consists of natural materials found at your chosen location. If you can find a fallen tree in just the right place, or a big stump to use as a backdrop, you just about have your blind made for you. Above all, plan your blind so you have a stump, tree trunk, or dense brush behind you to eliminate any hint of your silhouette. Then, if necessary, cut branches or brush to place in front to conceal you from approaching animals. Add enough cover so you are fully hidden in shadows; sunlight shining into the blind will highlight even your slightest movements and alert deer to your presence. Finally, trim out branches and twigs to assure clear shooting lanes in several directions. It should go without saying that full camouflage, including hands and face, is essential in a natural blind.

Many hunters favor commercial pop-up blinds over natural blinds, and for good reason. Good blinds like all the Double Bull models and the Ameristep Doghouse are light in weight, they set up in mere minutes (or seconds), and they assure absolute concealment as well as scent containment. Although additional cover generally is unnecessary, you can enhance concealment by stacking brush and limbs around and over the blind.

In selecting a commercial blind, always choose a model with a black lining. The darker the blind is inside, the less likely animals are to see you or detect your movements. Wear dark camo to blend into the shadowed interior of the blind. Also, because deer shy away from the black holes formed by open windows, select a blind with shoot-through netting over the windows. You can clearly see through the netting, but deer cannot see in. When the time comes, you can shoot right through the netting, which will not affect arrow flight.

*A blind with a camouflage cover secured over the PVC-pipe frame. Note that in some states and on some properties, pit blinds are illegal. In those cases you must use strictly above-the-ground blinds.*

# Other Species

Again, all of the general principles above regarding stand hunting, whether tree stand or ground blind, apply to all species of big game. Only the specifics of the habitat vary.

***Mule Deer:*** In contrast to whitetails, which you normally scout by analyzing sign in dense country, most mule deer live in open country, where you can scout visually. To identify good stand sites, get to a good vantage point, pick out a buck you want to hunt, and watch his movements for a couple of days until you detect a pattern. Good binoculars and a spotting scope are essential tools here.

Commonly you will see a buck travel through a saddle on a high ridge. Or you might see him follow a general route through an aspen patch or other timber. If you see him follow the same pattern a couple of times, you can assume that might be a good place for a stand. In many cases, you might find good stand trees there. If not, construct a ground blind or place a pop-up blind there.

In many cases, you can drive mule deer successfully. On a late hunt in Idaho, Cliff Dewell and I saw a buck feeding on an open hillside, and we tried stalking him there. When we accidentally bumped him, he trotted straight to the top of the hill and crossed through a saddle to the back side of the hill. Two days later we saw the same deer feeding on the same open hillside. This time, rather than stalking him, we decided I should circle around the back of the hill and take a stand in the saddle, and then Cliff would spook the buck toward me.

The plan worked to perfection. The only trouble was, a small buck came through the saddle first, and being a little string happy, I shot him. To my dismay, the big buck showed up seconds later. Although I'd goofed, the plan to take a stand in the saddle worked perfectly.

For mule deer living in arid desert and prairie habitat, water-hole stands may be even surer bets. If you can find an isolated water source — a spring or stock tank — with a good number of deer tracks around it, you may have found the perfect place for a blind. Again, use your pop-up blind, or, if cover is adequate, build a natural blind. In some places, a pit blind might be the best solution.

***Antelope:*** The key to antelope hunting in August and September, when most archery seasons are open, is water. Antelope water every day, and unlike deer, which might travel and water at night, antelope are diurnal, so you can count on their watering during daylight hours.

Antelope are the most visible of big game, so with a good spotting scope you can scout out the best bucks from long range. Once you've located some good bucks, try to determine where they're watering. If you don't actually see any animals visiting a water hole, drive or walk to all the water sources in the area and check for tracks. When you've found the most likely water holes, place your blind there. In the past, standard procedure was to dig a pit blind and to surround it with brush. Digging pits is now illegal in some states, and, it's a lot of work. For these reasons, a lot of antelope hunters are now going strictly to pop-up commercial blinds.

I mentioned the importance of a black interior in a blind, and that's especially true for antelope. With their extraordinary vision, antelope can see right into a blind from 200 yards away. But if the inside of the blind is black, and you wear dark camo, they will not see you. A black interior is the key to making any blind work for antelope.

Across the prairie states, many water sources are created by windmills, and the windmills themselves create excellent blinds. You can tie a sheet of cardboard or plywood to the framework of the windmill to break up your silhouette, but you don't need to be totally hidden. When you're 10 to 12 feet above the ground, antelope largely ignore you. As I sat on a windmill in Colorado, a buck antelope circled downwind of my stand and stared for long minutes. I believe he both smelled and saw me up there. Yet he still came in for a drink.

**Elk:** Fresh sign is the key to placing a stand for elk. To see why, contrast the nature of elk to whitetails. In good whitetail country, you will find tracks and other forms of sign just about anywhere there is adequate cover and feed. The presence of tracks alone doesn't indicate a good stand site.

Elk hunting is different. In any given mountain range, 70 to 80 percent of the land probably will contain no elk, nor elk sign. So you try to find the 20 percent with fresh sign. That's where you put your stand. Of course, certain kinds of sign make the best stand sites. Fresh wallows are always good bets. Just make sure you emphasize the word fresh. If the water is muddy and the tracks are new, a wallow is a good place for a stand. If the water has cleared and the tracks have faded, don't waste your time putting a stand there. Because elk commonly live in forests, you generally can use tree stands for elk. But in arid country, ground blinds as described above may be your only option.

In dry country, particularly throughout the Southwest, water sources are the primary focal points for tree stands. In Arizona and New Mexico, I would guess 70 to 80 percent of the elk taken by bowhunters are shot at water sources, particularly livestock tanks, springs, or catch basins in rock formations. The only problem with these places is that competition among hunters for the good spots can be pretty stiff.

Fence crossings are always good bets for stands. Elk commonly will follow fences for long distances until they come to a spot where the top strand is broken or loose. That's where they jump the fence. Stands downwind of such crossing points can produce close shots.

In some places, nutritious minerals lie near the surface of the earth, and elk (deer too) will actually eat the soil to ingest the minerals. These mineral licks are obvious from the tracks and trails leading to them, and the obvious hole where the animals have dug out the soil. Mineral licks can be excellent stand sites for elk.

Finally, heavily used trails between bedding and feeding grounds can produce results. Just make sure the trails are cut with fresh tracks. If the sign is not fresh there, look for other places with fresh tracks.

*Windmill blinds can be deadly for antelope. Even though you may not be well hidden up there, the antelope don't seem to recognize you as danger.*

*Chapter 8*

# Hunting on Foot

Straight ahead, about 20 yards through the brush, I noticed a white spot jiggling near the ground. *What is that?* I wondered. In the shadows of the rainy forest, it almost seemed to glow as it danced about, and for a minute or so I just stared, transfixed, trying to figure out what it was.

Then the buck raised his head, and I realized I'd been watching the white stripe over the tip of his nose as he'd nibbled grass and leaves in the thick brush.

I'd seen heavy deer sign in this pine grove, and with the intermittent rain and moist ground, footing was quiet. So rather than putting up a tree stand, I'd decided to still-hunt across the grove. I'd been moving slowly, a single step at a time, for about a half-hour, when I spotted the mysterious dancing white spot.

In the dense brush, I had no clear shot, so I simply stood motionless until the buck returned to feeding. Then, I slowly extracted an arrow from my quiver and fitted it onto the string. And waited. The buck gradually fed uphill until he entered an opening through the brush, 15 yards from me. That's where I shot him.

*Under some conditions, still-hunting can be the best way to hunt a number of different species. Gary Nichols took this fine Kansas whitetail while still-hunting along the cottonwood bottom in the background.*

Stand hunting has become so dominant among bowhunters that many no longer consider hunting on foot. One time, while hunting in Alabama, I suggested to my host that I might still-hunt through a stand of mature oak trees. There was no underbrush, the damp ground made for quiet footing, and the deer were moving well. To me it seemed a perfect situation for hunting on foot. But my host was adamant — it would not work. The only way to kill a deer was sitting in a tree stand.

That's too bad, because hunting on foot not only adds challenge and excitement to bowhunting, but in some situations it's simply the best way to hunt. If you don't learn and perfect methods for still-hunting, stalking, and calling, the three major approaches to hunting on the ground, you're only limiting your bowhunting skills and potential for success.

## Still-Hunting

Hunting on foot is far more than random walking through the woods. It's a technique with just as much structure and purpose as hunting from a tree stand. Under some conditions, it's not only the best way to hunt, but it can be the best way to hunt a number of species.

In the story that opens this chapter, I was hunting whitetail deer, and in many situations, still-hunting works very well for whitetails. But it's equally well suited to other forest species, too, especially mule deer and elk when other methods aren't producing. Success simply hinges on picking the right conditions and executing a plan. The beauty of still-hunting is that it's not only a good way to kill deer or elk, but it's a good way to scout during the season. If your stand location goes sour and you want to scout, but you don't want to waste hunting time, still-hunting is the way to go, because you can hunt and scout at the same time.

That was exactly the situation for me one late season in northern Idaho. Sitting in my stand, I had seen no deer all morning and wanted to scout for some fresh sign. The woods were damp, and on the mossy ground I was able to slip through the open forest as quiet as a cat. With a six-pound Trailhawk climbing stand strapped to my pack, I was creeping up a mossy little ridge when I saw two deer — a doe obviously in heat followed by a huge buck obviously in rut — about 80 yards uphill from me. At that point I had to decide whether to sneak up on them or climb a tree and wait. As they disappeared into a brushy draw, I decided — climb a tree now! Ten minutes later I was 15 feet up a tree and pulling up my bow. A half-hour later the big buck stood broadside, 35 yards from my stand. Although I was in a stand, it was still-hunting that put me into position to kill the biggest whitetail of my life. Too bad I shot under him.

***The Right Conditions:*** I recommend that you focus your still-hunting efforts on times when animals will be moving naturally: early and late in the day when deer are feeding and active; during the peak of the rut, when they likely will be active all day. Your chances for creeping up on animals bedded in dense brush where they not only are well hidden but where you can't move through the brush quietly are remote at best.

The right weather conditions are equally important. Even if you're hunting in a good area at the right time, if the ground is covered with dry maple leaves, frosty grass, or crusted snow, you won't sneak within bow range of many deer or elk. Those conditions call for hunting from a stand, not for still-hunting.

But when a soft rain is falling or a cool fog has settle in and the ground is sponge quiet, never ignore the potential for hunting on the ground. Light, soft snow creates good conditions, too. My friend Neil Summers, who lives in western Oregon, would not consider wasting a snowy morning by staying home. He will be out sneaking up on blacktail deer. Of course, fresh deer tracks in the snow give him valuable guidance, and his approach might more accurately be called tracking, but it still incorporates all the elements of still-hunting.

Wind can also be an ally in still-hunting. Even if the ground is dry and crunchy, you can get away with a lot when a blustery wind is kicking up leaves and groaning in the treetops. Hunters in corn-growing country even still-hunt for deer bedded in cornfields on windy days, because the deer can't distinguish the sound of the hunters rustling through the cornstalks. When the wind is blowing parallel to the rows, they start at the downwind end of the field and ease across the rows, peering up each row into the wind. If they cross the field without seeing a deer, they move into the wind 30 yards or so and hunt back across the field. They repeat this process until they have covered the whole field.

Of course, the subject of wind brings up the most critical criterion for still-hunting — a steady, reliable wind. If the wind is swirling, you're pretty much defeated before you start. That's one reason I like still-hunting in the prairie states. Every time I have hunted there, the wind has blown steadily in one direction for days at a time. In South Dakota, I saw a buck and some does enter a cottonwood grove along a river. The wind was blowing absolutely steadily from the west. So I went to the east end of the grove and slowly eased to the west. The lightly falling snow blew into my face with no variation in direction, keeping my confidence high. And it wasn't long before that buck and I met in a face-off. I won that one.

*To make still-hunting work, you must pick the right conditions. When a soft rain is falling or a cool fog has settled in and the ground is sponge quiet, never ignore the potential for hunting on the ground.*

**Equipment:** I've already covered clothing in detail, but a few additional thoughts are in order, because clothing is critical in still-hunting. You must be able to move freely and quietly so clothing must be soft, quiet, and nonrestrictive, and it must breathe well so you don't overheat. Heavy, lined garments designed to keep you warm, dry, and odor free in a tree stand won't work well on the ground. You're far better off wearing several light, unlined garments. Not only is each garment more pliant, but you can shed or add garments as needed. If it's a cool day, wear light silk or Thermax longjohns, and over that add wool or fleece, in light or heavy versions.

Heavy, insulated boots designed for sitting in a tree stand, or heavy hiking boots with stiff lug soles, are not ideal for still-hunting. You must be able to roll your feet silently into the ground with each step and to feel the ground as you move. In warm weather, I like shoes like Cabela's Scent-Lok Sneakers, which are essentially camouflaged tennis shoes. In cooler weather, leather-top, rubber-bottom boots like L.L. Bean's Maine Hunting Shoe with chain-link tread are ideal, because they have soft, pliable soles that allow quiet footfalls.

The right camouflage can be a major benefit in still-hunting, because you're moving at eye level with the game. As I've said elsewhere, pick camo patterns that blend with the environment you're hunting. In open hardwood forests, wear a medium-hue pattern like Advantage; in dark forests of spruce and fir, wear a darker pattern like Mossy Oak Breakup; in lighter timber, say aspens for elk, wear Predator Gray or ASAT; on snow wear a white, snow pattern.

In particular, camouflage your hands and face. On your hands, tight-fitting gloves are the best camouflage. In warm weather, light cotton gloves are good, and in cooler weather polypropylene gloves or wool military glove liners give good camouflage and keep your hands warm.

On your face, you can wear the same camo headnet you wear in a tree stand, but I personally prefer face paint. On the ground, you're constantly looking back and forth, and a face net can hinder your freedom. Also, I find that a headnet sometimes fogs my glasses. For these reasons I prefer — and recommend — camo face paint for hunting on the ground.

One final piece of equipment essential for peak still-hunting is binoculars. You might wonder what value powerful optics could have in short-range hunting. A low-power glass in the 6x to 8x range is invaluable for a couple of reasons: 1) The magnification helps you pick out details — an antler tine, a tail, an eye, the white line on a deer's nose — you would never see with your naked eye. 2) A low-power binocular with a large exit pupil gathers light, enabling you to see far better in dark woods and into deep shadows than you ever would with unaided eyes.

**Technique:** With the above preparation, you only have to develop your technique. Above all, never think of still-hunting as a way to walk through the woods and cover ground. That's scouting, or deer driving, or simply walking. But it is not still-hunting.

Still-hunting is literally mobile stand hunting. Once you enter into the core of your hunting area, you quit walking. Now you take one or two steps, rolling each foot carefully and silently into the ground. Then you stop and watch. Think about it this way: One reason hunting from a tree stand is so deadly is that you are sitting still as animals are moving. You will virtually always see them before they see you, and that's the basis for all successful bowhunting.

The principle is the same in still-hunting — the more time you spend motionless, the better your chances of seeing animals before they see you. Thus, you must stand still — on stand — for long periods, watching. If you're unable to see into shadows or brush, inspect these areas with your binoculars. If you see nothing in a minute or two of watching, take another two or three cautious steps and go on stand again. During this process, try always to stay in the shadows where you're least visible as you're moving. And when you stop to watch, stand in front of a

tree trunk, brush, or other solid cover where you are not silhouetted.

**The Results:** Hunting elk in northeastern Oregon, I was into good sign but could not get a bull to bugle to save me. One drizzly afternoon I headed up a dense north slope where I'd seen some heavy elk sign. With the rain, footing was silent. In an hour I'd moved scarcely 50 yards, spending most of my time watching and listening.

As I stood motionless in the shadows, I heard a slight clunk! *What was that? Maybe an elk hoof?* I wondered. With an arrow nocked, I remained still, eyes and ears focused ahead. Seconds later I heard leaves rustling. *Yes, there is something there.* I took three cautious steps and stopped in front of a tree trunk.

After tense seconds, I saw movement 35 yards away and raised my bow. As a cow elk stepped into the open, I simply had to draw and release and, after a short tracking job, recover my prize. Experiences like that are why I still hunt by still-hunting.

## Spot and Stalk

While still-hunting and spot-and-stalk hunting have many similarities, they also have major distinctions. Still-hunting is generally suited to areas of close cover with limited visibility, while spot-and-stalk hunting is tailored to desert, prairies, and

*In still-hunting, as in all hunting, steady wind is mandatory. I saw this South Dakota buck enter a cottonwood grove with the wind blowing steadily from the west. I went to the east end of the grove and met the buck halfway.*

*Above all, when hunting on the ground, camouflage your hands and face. You can wear the same style headnet you would wear in stand hunting, but many bowhunters, like Doug Chase shown here, prefer face paint because it's less restrictive.*

alpine areas, particularly in the West, where you can see long distances. Opposed to still-hunting, in which you're stalking "blind" for animals you have not yet seen, in spot-and-stalk hunting, you see animals first.

Spot-and-stalk hunting is probably associated most closely with mule deer, Coues deer, Sitka deer, bighorn sheep, mountain goats, and caribou, but other western species like elk, black bears, and moose, are often effectively hunted by stalking. And even whitetails are prime stalking targets in the right circumstances. I took one of my largest whitetails by stalking him in an open burn in central Idaho. And bowhunters regularly spot rutting bucks bedded in the sage or grass of the prairie states and stalk them successfully. Thus, spot-and-stalk hunting is not governed so much by the species as it is by the terrain and vegetation. Anywhere you can view an expanse of land to spot animals before they spot you, stalking tactics will work for you.

**Spot Your Game:** If you can't see animals, you can't stalk them, so spotting ability is perhaps your most valuable skill in hunting any game of the open country. The very definition of spot-and-stalk hunting means you see animals first from a distance, and then sneak up on them. In other words, in stalking, as opposed to still-hunting, you're sneaking up on animals you've already located. You could also stalk animals you've located by sound, such as a bull elk bugling across a canyon. But in most cases, spot and stalk starts with seeing animals at a distance. Five elements comprise good spotting:

**Optics:** High-quality binoculars in the 7x to 10x range are the core of the system. Compact binoculars may be okay for quick-checking details from a tree stand, but for stalking they're a severe hindrance. Among other shortcomings, they do not gather enough light for serious spotting, especially under dim light conditions. If you're serious about spotting game, you will never regret buying quality 7x36, 8x42, or 10x42 binoculars. My personal favorite for all-around hunting is the Bausch &

Lomb 8x42 Elite, but many serious western hunters prefer 10x binoculars.

For desert and mountain hunting where visibility may be measured in miles, a scope can be an invaluable addition to your spotting system. With 10x binoculars, you might spot animals two or three miles away, but you won't be able to tell how big they are. With a spotting scope, you can dial them in to see whether they're animals you really want to go after. In short, a scope will save you a lot of walking. A variable in the 15-45x range is great for all-around game evaluation. Without question, the best scope I've ever used is a Leica Televid 62 with a 16-48x eyepiece. I prefer an angled eyepiece rather than straight, because I can view objects to the side by just rotating the scope instead of moving my tripod. To get the most from a scope, you must mount it on a solid tripod. Scopes have got a bad rap for causing eye strain because you look with only one eye. To help ease eye strain, cover your off-eye with a dark cloth. The only problem with a quality, full-size scope is weight. For packing off-road, a lightweight fixed-power 20x or 25x scope will be far more comfortable.

Many serious game spotters use 15x to 20x binoculars mounted on a tripod — the ultimate spotting system. This system got its start with Coues deer hunters in Arizona. Although they live in fairly open terrain, Coues deer are small, about half the size of "normal" whitetails, and their mouse-gray hides blend perfectly with gray desert terrain. Coues deer hunters had to perfect the art of game spotting, and they have found that 15x to 20x binoculars are the best. Some popular models are the Swarovski 15x56, Zeiss 15x60, and Docter-Optic 15x60.

The heart of this spotting system is a good tripod. A high-quality tripod is well worth the money. Even the slightest jiggling nullifies the value of binoculars, and a tripod eliminates that, and you can set your binoculars on a tripod and look comfortably for hours. Even if you use 8x or 10x binoculars for your primary spotting tool, you'll see more game with the binoculars on a tripod. With a tripod, you can sit comfortably for hours, glassing systematically and efficiently. Most binoculars of 15x and higher come with tripod adaptors. For lower-power glasses, I use an adaptor that attaches with Velcro around the binocular and then screws onto a tripod.

**Place:** You need vantage points where you can see into good game areas. In the

*Spotting and stalking is most closely associated with species of the open country, like this mountain goat I killed in Idaho. I first spotted this billy from about a mile away and shot him four hours later at a range of 30 yards.*

alpine or desert, you may sit on a peak where you can see three miles in every direction. In more broken or timbered country, you might spot from a rim or hill where you can see only 100 yards. To kill one of my best bucks, I sat on a cliff looking down into an alder thicket. Visibility was 100 yards at best. But from that high point I could see two bucks feeding in the alders, and with that starting point, sneaked into the alders and got one of them.

Look for places you can get into without being seen. It does no good to sit watching if you've just walked through the country where you expect to see game. To prevent being seen, try to get into spotting position before daylight. And always stay off the skyline. Open-country animals live by their eyes, and will easily spot you on the skyline at distances of three or four miles. Sit and glass with trees, brush, or rocks behind you so you are not sky-lined.

**Time of Day:** By far, the best time for spotting deer and elk is right at daybreak. These species generally emerge from cover at dusk, feed during the night, and then retreat to cover shortly after sunrise. The time they're easiest to spot is right after sunrise, when they're still feeding in the open. That's another strong reason to be in spotting position before daybreak. Once they have bedded for the day, your chances for spotting them are greatly reduced.

However, you sometimes can spot mule deer in desert and prairie country during the day by inspecting bedding areas for antler tips. And the animals will get up to stretch and feed periodically throughout the day. So don't give up just because you don't see any stalkable animals right at daylight. Keep looking.

Diurnal (daytime) species like bighorn sheep and antelope will move throughout the day, so plan to spend all day behind your binoculars. Black bears, too, feed periodically throughout the day. In hot weather, however, even diurnal species seek relief from the sun in shady areas and will be difficult to spot in midday heat. So your best spotting could still take place early and late in the day.

**Duration:** A quick glance here and there won't spot you much game. You must devote time to looking and watching. If you spend only a few minutes at each spotting location, you'll overlook at least 50 percent of the animals available for stalking.

One January I hunted with Rusty Ulmer, a fanatical Coues deer hunter in Arizona. We took up our spotting positions at sunrise and were still sitting in that same place at sunset, looking through binoculars, 11 hours later. Duwane Adams, a famous Coues and mule deer guide, said he often spends all day looking from one vantage.

Isn't that much time spent in one place a waste of time? Not at all. That's especially true for species like Coues deer, which are very hard to spot under the best of conditions. For one thing, animals may be lying concealed, and if you glass for only a short time, you'll never see them. But if you glass for several hours, chances are good at least one animal will move, making him visible.

For another, with impatient glassing you'll overlook details you'd see with more patient study. Hunting mule deer one August, I'd twice seen a buck in a draw right at sunset, but in the mornings I couldn't find him. The only cover was a small wild plum patch, and I doubted the buck could hide in there. But after two mornings of his disappearing on me, I continued studying those plum bushes for more than two hours. Finally, I made out a black spot. It was the buck's nose. That buck had lain in there every morning, and I had overlooked him. Spotting takes time.

That doesn't mean you should always spend all day glassing from one spot. For desert mule deer or bighorn sheep, I commonly glass for a couple of hours from one vantage. If I see nothing in that time, I move to get a different angle and spend the next couple of hours glassing from my new position, and so forth throughout the day. The fact is, you simply cannot spend too

*High-quality binoculars in the 7x to 10x range are the very core of any spotting system.*

*In spotting animals for stalking, distances are sometimes measured in miles. To locate and evaluate big game at such distances, a good spotting scope like this Leica Televid 62 is priceless. The angled eyepiece is more versatile than a straight eyepiece. Always mount your spotting scope on a tripod.*

much time glassing. The outcome of your hunt hinges on your ability to spot game.

**Comfort:** If you're cramped, cold, and cranky, you'll never spend the requisite time spotting. If you're sitting on sharp rocks, you're cold or hot, or you're hungry and thirsty, you'll never last. Hiking to a spotting point in Arizona, Rusty Ulmer, with his overstuffed backpack, looks like he's going on expedition. He carries a huge down coat, a foam seat pad, and adequate food and water for the day (and, of course, his spotting gear). Those comfort items give him staying power.

To sit comfortably, carry a light folding stool or foam pad. And as Rusty Ulmer does, carry clothes for the conditions. Even Arizona can get frigid in January, and when you aren't moving around, you'll get cold in a hurry. To glass for long periods, you must be comfortable.

**Plan Your Stalk:** Once you've located a buck you want to stalk, be patient. Occasionally you may be able to stalk feeding bucks and will want to get on them immediately, but in most cases, you're best off to wait for a deer to bed for the day. That way he's stationary and you will have several hours to get within range, and while lying down, the deer will be looking mostly in one direction, which allows you to come in from his blind side. Also, in mountain country, the thermals will be blowing uphill during midday, so stalking down from above keeps the wind in your face — the one essential element common to all successful stalks.

As you're waiting for the deer to bed and the thermals to change, use your binoculars to plan a stalking route. Once you start your stalk, everything will look completely different, and you may very well not be able to find the animal you're after. Even in open sagebrush or prairie grass, relocating an animal at close range is one of the hardest parts of stalking. So study the area around the deer through your binoculars or scope, and note some solid landmarks to guide you as you move in. I often go so far as to pull out my notebook and draw a rough map.

Above all, assess the wind. Through your optics, study grass or bushes around your quarry to figure out precisely which way the wind is blowing. If possible, you want to approach from straight downwind. At the very least, plan a crosswind approach. As you plan, take plenty of time to locate other animals around the one you want to shoot. If you walk into an unseen animal, you'll start a stampede, and your stalk is over.

Finally, if you have a partner, work out some hand signals. This can be your most valuable aid in sneaking within bow range of an animal. Stalking a Coues deer in Arizona, I was sure the deer lay somewhere within 50 yards of me, but I simply could not see him. With binoculars, I looked back across the canyon to my partner, Rusty Ulmer. Motioning with his arm, Rusty indicated that the deer was bedded 30 yards to my right. Thirty yards? That didn't seem right to me, but trusting Rusty's signals — after all, he had a far better vantage of the overall situation than I did — I used my binoculars to take apart the brush there twig by twig — and finally spotted an antler tine. I eventually killed that buck, but I would never have got him without the helpful hand signals of a hunting partner.

***Move In:*** As in any bowhunting situation, clothing and footwear are critical in stalking. Refer back to "Still-Hunting" for suggestions on dressing for the final stages of a sneak.

I would add only a couple of thoughts on silencing your feet. To improve on lightweight footwear, slip fleece boot covers over your shoes. And for the ultimate in stealth (conditions permitting), take off your shoes and stalk in your sock feet. I often carry an extra pair of heavy wool socks to cushion my feet.

To stay hidden, wear head-to-toe camouflage that blends with your surroundings. In open terrain, many modern camo patterns are too dark, and they turn you into a black silhouette against light sage or grass. Far better are light-hued patterns like Predator Gray, ASAT, or military desert camo.

Even more important than the camo pattern you wear are how and where you move. Utilize any solid cover you can find. Keep cliffs and hills between you and your quarry as long as possible, and stay behind rocks and tree trunks wherever possible. Stalking mule deer on a treeless sagebrush flat, crawl on your hands and knees or belly to stay below the brush or grass line. For caribou on open tundra, use any small terrain feature to stay out of their sight. For deer, bighorns, or mountain goats in cliffs, get above them and use rocks and cliffs as cover.

In Colorado I spotted a band of eight bighorn rams feeding in an open tundra bowl. The only cover was a low rise. Late in the morning the sheep bedded on the south side of that rise. I circled around and approached from the north. To stay out of sight of those rams, I had to belly-crawl the last 100 yards to that rise, and when I got near the top and raised my head a few inches, I could see horns just over the top, 15 yards away. *Yipes!* That's close. I ended up shooting one of the rams at 25 yards.

Above all, stay off the skyline. Animals can spot movement on the horizon from miles away, and even though they may not immediately run, they will be alert and suspicious, which makes them doubly hard to stalk. Finally comes time. If you take enough time, your movement is virtually indiscernible to animals. And moving slowly, you can watch where you place your hands and feet for maximum silence. Stalking success can be summarized in one word — time.

***Make the Shot:*** Most stalks are blown for one of two reasons: Hunters get impatient and

*If you have a partner, work out some hand signals for the final stages of a stalk. This can be your most valuable aid in sneaking within bow range of an animal. Here, Rusty Ulmer demonstrates hand signals that directed me to a Coues buck.*

move too fast; or they try to get too close. I've covered the subject of too fast above, but what's this about getting too close?

You can get too close. The closer you get, the more likely an animal is to sense your presence, and the more explosively it will react. Also, the closer you get, the more intense the situation and the more nervous you get. Rather than pushing closer and closer until you can get a shot, you're far better off to get within your effective range and to stop. If your sure-kill range is 30 yards, get that close; if it's 20, get there and stop; but if it's 40 yards, stop there. Then wait for the animal to stand and present a shot.

If you've stalked up on a bedded mule deer, for example, settle in and wait for the deer to stand up on its own to feed or stretch. That will give you by far your best chance at a calm, unaware animal. If the wind seems squirrelly, you may need to make something happen before the animal smells you. I've had success flipping rocks off to the side to make an animal stand up. But you have to be careful with this. One windy day I tried flipping rocks, but the buck could never hear the rocks hitting the ground. So I tried throwing closer to the deer and accidentally hit him in the back of the head. I didn't get that one.

If a buck is moving, say feeding or rutting, get within reasonable range and wait for him to move into good shooting position. Once you're within bow range, you have no leeway for mistakes. Thus, just as in stand hunting, you have much the best chance if you're standing or sitting still and letting the animal come to you.

The emotional pressure of stalking can be overpowering. When you're sitting 15 feet above the ground in a tree stand, you can look down on animals with almost calm detachment, almost like God. But when you're sitting, crouching, or lying at eye level with a big game animal, and close enough to hear him breathing, the atmosphere is electric, making you feel all too mortal. It's a great feeling, the essence of bowhunting. And if you can control your emotions long enough to make the shot, you will have mastered one of the toughest but most productive of all bowhunting systems.

# Calling

Calling employs aspects of both still-hunting and spotting and stalking. However, it adds another dimension to these methods, and it greatly improves your odds for some species.

While calling — rattling, grunt calling, doe bleating, and so forth — can be just as effective at pulling whitetails within range on the ground as from a tree stand, it is not nearly as effective a way for killing them. That's because you're generally calling whitetails and blacktails in heavy cover, and the deer come in silently.

The first deer I ever rattled in was a blacktail in Oregon. Hidden in a clump of heavy ferns, I rattled for a couple of minutes and then sat quietly, watching and listening. Suddenly I noticed the eyeball of a deer, less than 15 yards away, staring at me through a hole in the brush. The deer peered for a half-minute and then evaporated

*When you spot an animal you want to stalk, don't get in a hurry. Take plenty of time to analyze the situation and to plan your stalk. If necessary, draw yourself a rough map.*

into the dense forest. I'd rattled in a buck but had absolutely no potential for a shot.

That's typical of calling deer on the ground, and it demonstrates why I recommend calling deer only from a tree stand. On the ground, you can call in plenty of deer, but you'll rarely, if ever, get a clean shot.

In contrast, calling on the ground can be the best way to hunt animals like elk and moose. Shear size is one reason. Elk and moose are so big you're likely to see them coming, even in dense brush. And even if you can't see them, you'll probably hear them. During the rut, they're aggressive and often approach with little caution. They will break branches, and often you can hear their heavy hoof beats on the ground. And, of course, bull elk bugle and bull moose grunt, so in most cases you will hear them calling. These warnings tell you where the animals are, and they give you time to prepare for a shot.

Similar principles apply to calling all animals on the ground — deer, turkeys, predators, hogs, javelinas — but for simplicity I will focus on elk and moose here.

***Time of Year:*** For best calling you must hunt during the rut. Generally, you can call in elk anytime during September. Many hunters think the peak of the rut — from September 20-25 in most areas — is the best time, but I've always had good calling success in early September, too. For moose, I've had best calling success between September 20 and October 10.

***Types of Sounds:*** Elk make two primary vocal sounds: During the rut, bulls make a high-pitched whistling sound called bugling, accompanied by various grunting, chuckling, and braying sounds. All year long, elk communicate with high-pitched mewing and whining sounds. Hunters generally call this cow calling, but all elk make these sounds.

Bull moose in rut make low grunting sounds. Up close, this grunting seems subtle and quiet, but on a calm day you can hear bulls grunting from a half-mile or farther. Cow moose make whining, moaning, and groaning sounds that carry hundreds of yards through the woods. To learn these sounds, acquire videotapes of elk and moose hunting. Many excellent tapes are available these days.

In addition to these vocal sounds, bull elk and moose thrash trees with their antlers, and you often can hear the sounds of rubbing and breaking branches from hundreds of yards away. Most hunters generically call this raking, and it's a good addition to any calling scheme. For elk, you can just grab a big stick and thrash a bush or small tree with it. For moose, many hunters carry an empty, plastic, white, antifreeze container cut in half; the dried shoulder blade bone off a deer or elk; or a small shed moose antler for raking. These not only produce realistic raking sounds, but when flashed in the air they simulate the flash of a moose's antler palm.

***Locating Animals:*** For both species, the general approach is to hike through the woods, calling, until you get a response from a bull. For both species, both bull and cow sounds are good locator calls. Experiment. If you're hunting elk in a place you're sure contains some bulls, and bugling doesn't bring a response, try cow calling. Sometimes that will elicit a response when bugling won't. If those don't work, rake a tree. Often that will stir the ire of a bull when nothing else will. Try the same progression on moose — try grunting first, then cow moaning, and finally raking.

In terrain with varied topography, call from high points where your calling will carry some distance, and where you can hear animals from long range. Call from one point and then move to another point and call from there, and keep moving and calling until you hear an animal. If you hit some hot sign and feel confident animals are nearby, call there for a half-hour to an hour. Sometimes persistent calling will generate a response when sporadic calling will not.

In flat, dense terrain, where sound does not carry far, move fairly rapidly and call regularly. The idea is to get a response from a bull so you know his whereabouts before you walk into his territory and spook him.

***Setting Up:*** When you have heard a bull, you want to get close enough to call that animal to you. You could hear a bull from a distance of a half-mile or more, and in most cases you will not call him to you from that far away. He might stand over there and bugle or grunt at you for an hour but never move your way, because he doesn't feel threatened.

But if you move closer to make him think you have invaded his territory, his attitude will change, and he will probably come to challenge you — and present you with a shot. How close

*When hunting Elk in terrain with varied topography, call from high points where your calling will carry some distance, and where you can hear animals from long range. Keep moving and calling until you get a response from a bull.*

must you get? For moose and elk, I think 200 yards is more or less the critical range. Get within that distance and you probably will muster some action; stay farther away and you may not pull the animal to you.

By far, the most critical part of any setup is wind. Before you move toward an animal, check the wind with a dust bottle or other wind checker and move until the wind is blowing from the animal to you. Then move in.

As you move toward an animal, I recommend that you cease calling. At this stage, you want to find a good ambush before you start a bull coming your way. If you lose track of the bull and need to relocate him, then you might have to call to figure out where he is. Otherwise, remain quiet until you have blinded in, ready to shoot.

When you think you're 200 yards or closer, look for a place to hide and call. This is critical. Poor setups probably explain more calling failures than any other single aspect. Guys get in a hurry and start calling before they have really found a good ambush point, and they get caught off-guard and unprepared.

There is no set formula for calling success. Experiment with bugling, cow calling, and raking, and try different types of calls to produce different sounds. With some trial and error, you will find a sound that pushes a bull's hot button. Larry D. Jones carries a variety of calls to produce a variety of elk sounds.

**Every good setup has two elements:**

***Shooting Lanes:*** First, find a place where you can get a shot. It does no good to call in a bull if you can't get a clear shot, and in dense brush, you very well could call a bull within 15 yards or closer and still not get a shot. To prevent that frustrating situation, take time to search around until you find a small meadow, a break in the brush, or other small opening where you can shoot out to at least 20 or 25 yards. If necessary, cut out limbs or branches to create open shooting lanes in two or three directions. A knife or small saw will work, but I prefer a lightweight ratchet clipper, because it's quick and quiet.

***Good Concealment:*** Don't get behind heavy cover, because you'll have a hard time getting a clear shot. Rather, stand or kneel in front of cover, say a stump, tree trunk, or dense branches, so you're not silhouetted. Or back into the branches of a tree and trim limbs out of the way to give yourself shooting clearance. Always try to hide in dark shadows; in sunlight, your every move will be highlighted. Of course, full camouflage on body, hands, and face is important to complete any concealment system.

***Calling Him In:*** Only when you've completed your setup with adequate shooting lanes and concealment should you start calling again. How do you call in a bull? Normally, on elk, I start with quiet cow calling. If that seems to stir up the bull and get him coming my way, I stick with just that. If it doesn't seem to be working, then I'll get more aggressive by bugling and raking a tree. On moose, I normally start with some grunting and raking with a shed antler. If that doesn't work, I'll mix in some cow calling. I've had better success calling in moose with antler raking than with any other technique.

There is no set formula. Try one approach, and if that doesn't work, experiment until you hit a chord that pushes the bull's hot button. Also, try different brands and styles of calls. Even different styles of diaphragm calls will produce slightly different sounds — and possibly different responses from a bull. With persistence you'll find a sound or combination of sounds that will pull a bull to your position.

You can enhance a setup with the use of scents. Determine right where you want a bull to stop and place a scent dispenser laced with elk or moose scent there, just as you would do in a whitetail setup. You can also enhance an elk setup with a decoy or decoys to pull a bull into a particular shooting lane.

***Making the Shot:*** Of course, not every elk or moose will come to your calls. Some bulls with cows will simply move away to protect their breeding rights. Others might just hang up out of range and refuse to come your way out of fear or caution. Still others might see or smell you and vacate the premises.

But following the above approach, you will pull some bulls within bow range. From experience, I would say average shooting distance on moose and elk is 15-30 yards. The main ingredient in getting a good shot is patience. With a good setup — wind in your favor, good concealment, good shooting lanes — you don't have to hurry the shot.

Most animals coming to your calls will be coming head-on. Don't shoot. Always wait for a broadside or quartering-away shot. Scents or decoys can help divert the attention of an incoming bull to give you a broadside shot. But even without those aids, you will, with patience, get the right angle. Simply wait quietly and without moving. Sometimes bulls will get angry and begin raking a tree, giving you a great shot. Other times they will stroll on by your position in their search for their antagonist, and you can get a broadside shot. If an animal is walking too fast for you to shoot, draw your bow, wait until he enters a shooting lane, and give a quick cow call or grunt to stop him.

In some cases, a bull will get suspicious and turn to leave. If that happens, start calling again. Both elk and moose are vocal animals, and they instantly respond to calling. Often you can call a bull back in, even after he has spooked. So don't give up on calling until you're sure the bull has totally fled the area.

Or until you shoot. And even then you should be prepared to call. (For full details on shot selection and placement, see Chapter 9.) Generally, when your arrow strikes a bull elk or moose, the animal will bolt away. If you call loudly at that instant — bugle at an elk, cow moan at a moose — even a mortally wounded bull will stop to listen. And more often than not he will drop right there without taking another step. In some cases, this quick calling action can save you hundreds of yards of difficult trailing. And put you in a photo with the trophy of a lifetime.

*When a bull comes your way, be patient and wait for a good shot angle. A bull coming head-on does not present a good shooting angle. Wait until the bull is broadside like this.*

*Chapter 9*

# Aim to Kill

**A**s I stood there, with nothing but a 60-pound bow in my hand, watching a 1,500-pound bull moose charging my way, a question popped into my mind: "Can this flimsy stick and string kill something as big as a moose?"

I sure hoped so, although I didn't have much time to ponder the question as the beast thundered within 35 yards of me and slammed to a halt, glaring around to locate his lovesick cow. I aimed at a spot low on the bull's chest and released an arrow. For 10 seconds the woods became a pandemonium of crashing followed by utter silence. I moved forward to look around and found my first Alaskan moose lying 50 yards away. The answer was clear. The bow and arrow has the potential for killing any big game animal in North America quickly and humanely. You can trust your archery tackle — if you can trust yourself.

Obviously, clean kills begin with shooting accuracy, a subject covered in previous chapters. But the ability to hit a spot does no good if you don't know which spot to hit or when to hit it. That's what this chapter is about.

*As this moose crashed through the brush toward me, I had to ask myself, "Can this flimsy stick and string kill something as big as a moose?" The answer is obvious. With good shot selection and placement, a modern bow will cleanly kill any big game in North America.*

# The Right Spot

The only acceptable aiming point is one that will result in a double-lung or heart hit. Why? First, an arrow through both lungs or the heart will kill any animal within seconds. Whether you're hunting deer, elk, moose, or grizzly bears, a double-lung or heart hit guarantees a quick kill. Second, the heart-lung area offers some leeway in shot placement. Yes, you should aim for a specific spot, but if you hit 2 or 3 inches in any direction from that spot, you will still make a kill. The lung-heart area presents the largest kill zone on any big game.

On an animal standing broadside to you , you want to aim just behind the front leg, about one-third of the way up the chest. Horizontally, that centers your arrow on the lungs. (This assumes a broadside, ground level shot.) But why should you aim at a point one-third of the way up the chest rather than at the vertical center? Dr. Randy Ulmer, a veterinarian and Hoyt staff shooter, explained:

*By far, the best shot is a broadside shot on a calm, feeding animal like this. Aim a few inches behind the front leg and about one-third of the way up the chest. A shot through the lungs or heart will kill an animal quickly, and the heart-lung region presents the largest kill zone.*

"Hunters often assume if they shoot an arrow through both lungs, the lungs will collapse and kill the animal. But several layers of skin and muscle, which slide across each other, are stretched over the chest. If these seal an arrow hole quickly, the lungs won't collapse. Then the animal must die by hemorrhage.

"High in the chest, however, the lungs are thinner, and the blood vessels are relatively small. So an animal hit high in the lungs won't necessarily bleed to death. Contrary to what some hunters believe, there is no 'dead space' between the lungs and backbone. On a living animal, the lungs fill the entire chest cavity."

Keeping your aiming point low, then, assures that you will hit the blood-rich lower lungs. Let's assume you aim at the very center of the chest. If the animal is a little closer than you think, your arrow will strike high in the chest, and there's a very good chance you will not recover the animal.

However, let's make the assumption that you've aimed at a point one-third of the way up the chest. If you hit your mark, you've made a perfect kill. What if the animal is closer than you think and your arrow hits high? Your arrow will still hit the middle of the chest for a solid double-lung hit. And if the animal is a little farther than you estimate and your arrow hits low, the arrow will hit either the heart, which guarantees a quick kill, or will miss the animal completely, both of which are okay.

## The Right Angle

The above scenario assumes a broadside shot from ground level. I consider a broadside shot the best angle, because your arrow is most likely to pass completely through an animal at that angle. And that's what you want, because two holes are always better than one. They assure maximum damage and a generous blood trail. In the past, hunters commonly debated this point. Some thought it was better for an arrow to remain in an animal, because it would continue to "work" as the animal ran off. But these days, with the advent of high-power bows that commonly yield pass-through shots, most experienced bowhunters agree that pass-throughs produce the quickest, surest kills.

*Hold off on animals quartering toward or facing you. If you aim for the chest on this buck, your arrow will hit one lung at best. And the back of the neck is not an acceptable shot under any circumstances.*

That doesn't mean an angling shot is not acceptable. On an animal quartering away, you would simply move your aiming point back a few inches. Basically you aim at the front leg on the off side. If an animal is quartering sharply away, your aiming point would be right at the back of the rib cage.

If the angle is steeper than that, I recommend that you do not shoot, for a couple of reasons. One, your arrow has to travel through a lot of body to reach the vitals. With some bows that would be no problem, but with a moderate draw-weight bow, or with open-on-impact broadheads, that could be a problem. Two, because of the steep angle, your arrow can deflect off a rib and penetrate poorly, or slide along the outside of the rib cage and not enter the body cavity at all.

An animal quartering toward you does not present a good shot. Even if you hit close behind the front shoulder, the arrow, angling back through the body, will probably catch only one lung at best. Hold off on quartering-to shots. Wait for the animal to turn broadside.

From a tree stand or other high point, you must raise the aiming point higher onto the chest to assure that your arrow will angle down through both lungs. At moderate angles that's no problem. Just aim 3 or 4 inches above your normal, ground-level aiming point.

But as a deer nears your stand, the shooting angle becomes steeper and steeper until you're shooting nearly straight down at the deer's back. That's a tempting shot because the deer is close, but in reality this is one of the worst shots possible.

For one thing, from a high angle the arrow most likely will pass through only one lung, and, as Ulmer said, "A deer can live forever on one lung."

For another, on a steep downward shot, your arrow travels nearly parallel with the rib cage. If the arrow strikes to the side of the backbone, it likely will slide between the hide and ribs, pass neatly between the front shoulder and ribs, and bury itself in the ground, giving you the impression of a perfect pass-through chest shot when, in fact, your arrow has never entered the chest cavity. These problems with steeply angled shots present one argument for keeping tree stands relatively low, say 15 to 20 feet high, where you're assured of broadside shots — and clean kills.

# Shot Selection

*Timing:* As discussed above, the best angle is broadside or slightly quartering away. You should hold off on all other shot angles. But animal attitude is equally important. Shooting at a tense or an alert animal is nearly as ill advised as shooting at a bad angle or shooting beyond your effective range. That's because a tense animal is coiled, ready to spring.

That's where the old expression "jumping the string" comes from. When you release the bowstring, the bow produces a certain amount of noise. Because the average arrow travels at about 250 feet per second, and sound travels at about 1,100 feet per second, the sound of the bow reaches the animal about four times faster than the arrow. Thus, animals have an appreciable warning before the arrow arrives, and fleet animals like deer and antelope have such fast reflexes that even at distances as close as 20 yards they can move far enough to either create a bad hit or completely dodge the arrow.

The concept of string jumping generally suggests that animals only react to the sound of a bow. However, if they're alert and are looking at you, they will see movement as soon as your bow tips start forward. I think this is a bigger concern than their jumping at the noise, because they don't have to wait for the noise to reach them. They can respond instantaneously.

While string jumping is most common with small quick animals like deer and antelope, larger animals like elk have surprisingly quick reaction time. After all, all big game animals must survive many threats in the wild, friendly critters like mountain lions and bears, and if they lacked lightning reflexes they would not last long.

Whether animals react to the sound or sight of the bow really makes no difference. The fact is they can and they do. And while even a relaxed, feeding animal can jump the string, the likelihood is much lower than it is with a tense or an alert animal. That's why good hunting skills are essential to clean kills. To assure good, clean-kill hits, you must get animals within your effective range, draw your bow, and release without alerting your quarry.

*Distance:* Shot distance certainly has a bearing on clean kills. In part, it relates to your ability to hit your aiming spot. Clearly the farther the distance, the less leeway you have in terms of range estimation, accuracy, and outside influences like wind and obstacles. So there is a practical limit to how far you should shoot. In many cases that is simply limited by vegetation. In the average whitetail stand, you would be hard pressed to get an open shot beyond 20 yards, because branches, leaves, and tree trunks block your view beyond that distance. Even if you can shoot accurately out to 50 yards, a 25- or 30-yard shot might be irresponsible from a stand, because you might have little chance of making a clean hit beyond those yardages, regardless of your shooting ability. Your arrow will be deflected before it reaches the deer.

But let's say you're in a blind overlooking a desert spring in Nevada. It's a clear, calm morning, and a mule deer stands broadside, drinking, 50 yards from your ground blind. Would that shot be irresponsible? Not if you can shoot accurately out to that distance. In the desert terrain, no obstacles lie between you and the deer, and in the calm air your arrow will fly true. But what

From a tree stand, you need to adjust your aiming point higher to get a good double-lung hit. On this elk you would aim close behind the front leg and at the vertical center of the chest or slightly higher so your arrow will angle downward through both lungs.

if the wind is blowing 20 miles an hour? Would a 50-yard shot still be acceptable? No. Not only can you not hold your bow steady in a strong wind, but you can't gauge precisely how much your arrow will drift. A strong cross wind might reduce your responsible shot distance to 20 or 30 yards.

Another consideration in relation to distance is animal movement, which relates back to string jumping. Some experienced bowhunters would say that the farther the shooting distance, the more time an animal has to move or jump the string. That theory holds some truth, of course. Virtually any alert big game animal has the reflex speed to elude an arrow at 50 yards. Even if the animal does not jump the string, it could simply take a step during the time your arrow is in flight. One way or the other, the result is a bad hit.

That suggests, then, that the closer, the better. However, another school of thought would say that the closer an animal is, the more likely it is to jump the string because the more likely it is to see or hear you. In other words, this theory would say that a shot at a calm, feeding, unaware animal at 50 yards is better than a shot at a tense animal at 20. This concept holds a certain amount of truth, too. The bottom line is that no one can dictate an absolute maximum shooting distance for all archers. Effective range depends too much on individual ability and on conditions at the moment.

With all of that said, I will stick my neck out and offer some concrete guidelines based on my personal experience and on observing many other bowhunters over more than 30 years. For most traditional archers shooting barebow, myself included, I would say maximum range is 20 yards for the average shooter, 30 yards for the very best. For most compound archers using sights, I believe maximum responsible shooting distance lies somewhere between 30 and 50 yards. Beyond 50 yards the variables become so great that clean kills are not guaranteed.

And perhaps that's the bottom line: If you preface a shot with, "Maybe I can get one in there," don't shoot, regardless of distance. "Maybe" won't cut it. Shoot only when you can say to yourself, "I can make this shot. No doubt about it."

# Beating Buck Fever

Clearly I recall my first good shot at a bull elk. He was feeding down a draw, and I waited calmly in the shadows until he stood broadside at 15 yards. At that point I drew my 60-pound Kittredge recurve — and launched an arrow a foot over the elk's back. I later found that arrow about 50 yards out in a meadow.

Even if you have excellent shooting skills and practice restraint in picking your shots, you can make bad shots on game. The culprit is mental failure. Buck fever. A good practice regimen as discussed in Chapter 4 helps combat buck fever, because it builds an autopilot mode into your body. When a deer approaches, you don't have to think about making the shot. Through repetitive practice, you unconsciously do everything right. So good practice is the starting point.

Even at that, you can still lose mental control in heated moments and do dumb things — as I did on the bull elk. I didn't miss because I was not a good shot with the bow. Actually, I shot pretty well. No, I simply blanked out and mindlessly launched an arrow into space. So mental conditioning can be as valuable as shooting practice.

For starters, develop a routine. When I first got into bowhunting, an old-timer told me he always tipped his hat back, checked his hand position on the bow, and picked a spot before shooting at an animal. This little routine calmed him down. A professional archer told me he counts to 10 and takes a few deep breaths before taking a critical shot. I personally like to run through a quick mental checklist — bow-hand placement, stance, arrow on the rest, release aid on the string. These are all familiar steps that focus my mind rather than letting it run rampant. Any routine like this can help calm you before a high-pressure shot.

*No one can prescribe an exact maximum shooting distance, because it depends so much on conditions. You might consider yourself accurate out to 50 yards, but in forested or brushy country like this, 20 to 30 yards might be the maximum responsible shot distance.*

Certain shooting methods can also help. All mental breakdowns in archery could be lumped under the term "target panic." We won't debate here whether target panic and buck fever are the same thing, because the solutions can be identical. In general, the problem in target panic is anticipation of the shot, so the solution is "surprise," and any device that introduces an element of surprise into the shot can reduce the problem. The section "Beating Target Panic" in Chapter 4 offers several mechanical solutions for the target panic/buck fever disease.

Catchwords these days are visualization and imagery. Essentially, these mean you picture something strongly in your mind — like shooting an elk — so you will perform better when faced with the reality of doing that. The value may be overstated (by people selling books on visualization), but I think it does have some value, especially in an activity like shooting elk where you can't get regular practice. You can shoot 3-D elk targets or virtual-reality systems like the Dart system, and these do help. But they aren't the same as real encounters.

Unfortunately, the average hunter won't get more than one or two shots at big game each fall, so getting adequate, real-life experience is difficult. That's where visualization comes in. If you study photos or videos of big game, or you analyze live animals at the zoo and mentally picture yourself making perfect shots on those animals, you build images of success in your mind. Sit back, close your eyes, and see yourself placing arrows in the kill zone. Just as you train your body through repetitive form practice, you can train your mind through repetitive mental drills.

In 1999, almost 30 years after missing that first bull elk, I was hunting with a recurve bow again very similar to my original Kittredge. A friend and I had hunted for five days when we called in a cow elk. As the cow stopped broadside, I drew and released, and the elk ran only 100 yards before dropping. I suppose experience alone had something to do with my success, but so did my practice regimen and mental drills. I had practiced my shooting form for hours at home, building a solid, automatic style, and for the five days prior to calling in that cow, I had shot my bow constantly at rotten stumps and pine cones. In addition, I'd visualized myself many times drawing on elk, picking a spot right behind the front shoulder and placing an arrow right there. And before starting to call, I took time to find a good blind with clear shooting lanes. When I drew on that cow, my mind went blank, just as it had done on that bull 30 years earlier and has done on every elk since, but because of my preparation, the arrow flew true. Really, that's all there is to the killing shot.

# Game Recovery

If you follow all of the above steps, you will make good hits on animals more than 90 percent of the time, and you should see or hear your animals go down.

That's the key to game recovery — a good hit. I would say that, on average, animals hit through the heart or both lungs die in less than 30 seconds and travel somewhere between 50 and 100 yards. And that's true regardless of the size or speed of the animal. The first antelope I ever shot bolted at full speed and fell exactly 30 yards from the point at which it had been hit. Considering that antelope can hit speeds up to 50 miles an hour or more, you know that buck was dead in very short seconds. I've shot four moose, and none has traveled farther than 50 yards before going down. Make no mistake: A good hit is the real key to game recovery.

Even at that, you can't guarantee 100 percent perfect hits. At some point, if you bowhunt enough, you will have to trail a wounded animal some distance, in some cases a mile or more, and how you go about it will determine the outcome.

*Initial Steps:* Recovery begins the instant your arrow strikes an animal, and your first response may be the most critical. First of all, remain still and quiet. In many cases, animals hit with arrows have no idea where the arrow came from. Often they'll run, but in some cases they won't. If an

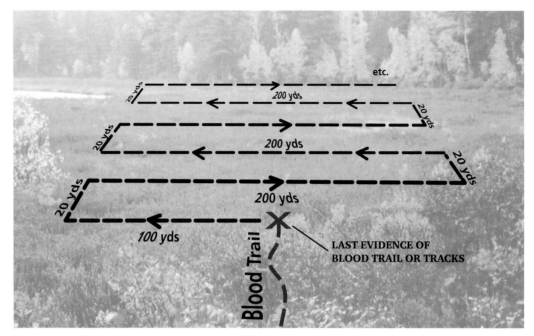

*This diagram shows the search pattern to use when you lose a blood trail. Mark the point where you lost the track and prepare to follow a broad sweep of the area. Using a compass or GPS to keep on course, search about 100 yards to one side of the trail, advance 20 yards, and search to 100 yards on the other side of the trail, making a systematic sweep.*

arrow passes cleanly through an animal, it might simply walk a short distance and fall. When I shot a moose in Idaho, my arrow disappeared into the shadows and I did not see the arrow hit. As the moose simply kept walking another 20 yards, I thought maybe I'd missed — until his legs turned to rubber and he went down. The arrow had sliced so cleanly through his heart, he scarcely reacted. And that's not unusual. If you remain quiet, an animal either may not run at all, or may run only a short distance before slowing to a walk. In such cases, recovery will be short and sure.

If you don't see an animal go down, you still could hear him hit the ground. When I shot a whitetail in Idaho, the deer ran out of sight, but I continued listening intently — and shortly heard a crash, the only clue I needed. I walked toward the crash and found the buck dead, wedged under a log, 80 yards from my stand.

With other animals, you'll hear a "death moan." Bears commonly groan several times as they're dying, and elk will do the same. Listen carefully for any telltale sounds that indicate that an animal is expiring.

Even if you don't see or hear an animal go down, your immediate reaction is critical. Focus on the details of the hit. In most cases, you'll see your arrow hit the animal, and you can gauge shot placement. If your arrow hits the paunch and the animal humps up and "tiptoes" away, you will follow up far differently from how you will if the arrow slices through the chest and the animal streaks away at a dead run.

If you're in open country, as you might be in hunting mule deer or antelope, do everything possible to keep the animal in sight. If you can run to a high point for a better view, get there as fast as you can, and watch your animal as long as possible. Binoculars are invaluable here. If an animal goes down or out of sight, mentally mark the precise location where you last saw it.

In forest or other cover, of course, most animals will disappear within a couple of bounds. Even at that, watch and carefully mark the precise spot where an animal disappears. As editor of *Bowhunter* magazine, I have received numerous stories about animal recovery (or failure). In many, the authors have described how they or their companions have not carefully marked the point where animals went out of sight and have then wasted much time searching in the wrong spot. If you simply stay calm and mark an animal's departure route carefully, you've made a good start in retrieving your animal.

**Follow-Up:** Your initial observations are the starting point for game recovery. Once an animal has gone out of sight, you can quietly approach the place where he stood when hit and examine the evidence, which will confirm or contradict your initial observations. And it will tell you how quickly to begin trailing your animal.

First you want to mark exactly where the animal was standing. Stick an arrow in the ground there, or hang a strip of plastic flagging on a branch. Then search for your arrow. It might still be in the animal, but if it has passed through, it will be lying on the ground nearby. It holds valuable clues. If the arrow is covered with bright, frothy blood from broadhead to nock, you know it has passed through the lungs. If it's covered with bright blood that is not frothy, it probably went through the heart.

Dark red, non-frothy blood probably indicates a liver or muscle hit. You often can distinguish the two by your observation as the arrow struck the animal. Hair on the ground is also a clue. If you're hunting deer and you find only short brown hair, you can assume the arrow hit the chest. If you find longer, white hair cut by the broadhead, you can assume you hit the deer around the fringes, either in the brisket or in a lower leg.

If a thin film of fat coats the shaft, but there is no blood, your arrow probably passed through the skin at the top of the back. That's a distinct possibility if the animal jumps the string. Actually, it would be more accurate to say "ducks the string," because as an animal coils to spring away, it drops down. If the arrow has only a little dark blood, along with green slime, and it has a bad odor, you can bet it passed through the paunch or guts.

All of this brings us to one of the more hotly debated questions: How long should you wait before trailing an arrow-hit animal? General convention says to wait at least a half-hour. That might be a good general guideline, but it's far from universal.

If you're confident of a solid chest hit and you find your arrow covered from end to end with bright blood, you probably have no need to wait. The same is true if you see or hear the animal hit the ground. As mentioned above, you will often hear a death moan or crash that tells you an animal is dead. In such cases, you have little reason to wait. If you actually see an animal fall, watch it for a while to see if it moves or is still breathing. The best place to recover an animal is in its first bed, so wait until you're sure it is dead before approaching. Binoculars are invaluable for this purpose, even for close-range woods hunting.

A few years back, I shot an elk late in the evening. The animal went about 50 yards and lay down. Because I'd been hunting for many days and was tired, I had done everything possible to decrease the weight of my daypack, which included leaving my binoculars in camp. Bad mistake. In the gathering darkness of the forest, I could not clearly analyze the bull's condition. As I watched with my naked eye, he appeared about done. So I stalked silently closer for a follow-up shot. But before I could get into position, the bull detected me and ran off into the dark forest. I eventually recovered that elk, but it took several hours and a mile of tedious trailing. With binoculars I could have inspected the elk in his initial bed and backed off. I'm sure he would have died right there if I had not given him a shot of adrenalin that carried him on a long, desperate run.

Because of situations like that I recommend that you never enter the woods without good,

*Binoculars are invaluable for recovering animals. They help you pick out details and peer into dark shadows to locate and analyze animals you're following.*

light-gathering binoculars. Even if you're just out for an afternoon on your Back 40, good optics are often invaluable in game recovery.

If you think the animal is hit "a little far back," as hunters often say, or a little high, then the best policy is to wait for at least a half-hour. The theory is that an animal that is mortally wounded, but that may not die for a few minutes, will run only a short way before lying down. If left alone, that animal will die in its first bed and will be easy to find. Chances are it will travel less than 200 yards, which should make it easy to recover. But if you get impatient and trail immediately, you could bump that animal in its first bed, and it could run several hundred yards farther on adrenaline alone. At that point it could be very difficult to find. If you have any doubt, play it safe and wait for a half-hour to an hour before trailing.

Now let's say you know for sure your arrow has hit an animal in the stomach or guts. Again, the half-hour waiting period does not apply. A gut shot animal will definitely die, but it could travel a long way — a mile or farther — before it does. And the more you push it, the farther it will go, and the harder it will be to find. To complicate the issue, the blood trail will be sparse to nonexistent. Thus, you want to do everything possible to let that animal die in its first bed. And to do that, you want to wait several hours before trailing. Five to six hours would be none too long. If you gut-shoot a deer in the morning, wait until late afternoon before trailing. If you shoot the deer in late afternoon or evening, simply return home or to camp, and come back the next morning to recover your deer.

**_Tracking and Trailing:_** Your most valuable trailing tool is your attitude. If you go at this with the attitude, "I will not quit this trail until I find that animal," you will succeed. Dedication is a self-fulfilling prophecy. That is, if you have the will to succeed, you will find the way to do it.

Before taking up the trail, clearly mark the spot where the deer was standing when your arrow struck. That point is always your starting point for your search. Then search for blood. Even on hard-hit animals, blood does not hit the ground for a number of yards. When you find the first drops, mark them. You can use an arrow to mark these spots, but you're probably wise to keep some fluorescent plastic flagging in your pack just for this purpose (always go back and retrieve all your flagging after you're done).

On a lung or heart-shot animal, you probably can walk upright and follow the blood at a brisk pace. But that's not always the case. If the arrow hit fairly high, most of the blood could remain inside the animal, leaving a sparse blood trail. And some muscle or abdominal hits will produce a poor blood trail. In these cases, you may have to crawl to stay with your animal. Get down on your hands and knees so your eyes are no more than a foot or so from the ground. You will see specks of blood you would never see from a farther distance.

For a half-mile or more, a friend and I trailed an elk he had hit. At first we were picking up a drop of blood every 10 feet or so, but eventually the blood just gave out. We circled for an hour or more but simply could not locate the trail. As we were almost ready to give up, I noticed a place where some deep pine needles had been disturbed. I crawled back and forth through these needles for 15 minutes and finally found a tiny speck of blood on one pine needle. That put us back on the trail, and we eventually recovered that bull.

Getting low also allows you to look up under leaves and blades of grass. Often blood will not drip to the ground but will soak down into an animal's fur. It will then smear onto the undersides of leaves and grass as the animal passes. Often you will do most of your trailing by following these smears rather than drops of blood.

While blood is your most valuable clue, other signs can keep you on the trail. When you take

*When a blood trail is scarce or nonexistent, study the tracks of the animal you're following. They could be your only clues. When I shot this bull elk in Wyoming many years ago, his hide slid over the arrow hole, eliminating any hope for a blood trail. But I was able to follow the tracks for nearly a mile to find my prize.*

up the trail of an animal, note the size and shape of its tracks. And note how fresh they look. Once you imbed these signs in your mind, you will quickly recognize the tracks of your animal as you follow the trail. Take special notice of any abnormalities. In Wyoming I shot an elk and my arrow passed through the chest and abdomen and lodged against the opposite back leg. The wound left no blood trail, but the bull dragged his back right foot. I recognized the drag marks and followed them through many other elk tracks for a half-mile or more and recovered the elk.

If you can't clearly see tracks, measure stride length, the distance from one track to the next, and use this as a gauge to locate tracks. Use one of your arrows or a stick as a measuring gauge. I once was having a hard time tracking a bull elk. There was no blood trail, and the tracks were obscure. So I used one of my arrows to measure from the front of one hoofprint to the back of the next — 28 inches. When the tracks occasionally faded on hard ground, I kept on the elk's trail by gauging the position of the next tracks with my measuring arrow. I followed the elk for several hundred yards by this method alone.

Also, always look for other clues like scuffed leaves, broken twigs, bent grass, disturbed water — anything that could mark the recent passing of an animal. These alone may not lead you to an animal, but they're all pieces of a larger puzzle that lead to a complete picture.

Above all, stay with the trail as long as possible. On a sparse trail, there's always a temptation to abandon the trail in favor of random searching. Don't do it. Keep working out the blood and other sign. They're your one link with the animal. Once you have lost these, you've lost much of your hope.

If two or more of you are working together, one person can stay with the trail while the other searches ahead, although the searcher must be careful not to trample valuable signs. Two people work well together, because they can encourage each other, and two sets of eyes see more than one. However, larger parties can be counterproductive, because several people can get in each other's way, and a competitive spirit can even develop. That hurts more than it helps.

Don't despair if night falls before you recover an animal. Unless an animal is gut shot, I suggest you keep on the trail into the dark. In fact, I'm not sure you can't blood trail better in the dark than in the daylight. At the least you need a good bright flashlight. A gas lantern works even better, but you need to wrap a foil reflector around one side to keep the light out of your eyes. Blood shows up very well in the focused beam of a flashlight or lantern. In addition, you're forced to get down closer to the ground and to move slower. As a result, you can trail very effectively in the dark.

If you finally lose a trail and simply can find no more clues — if all hope seems lost — then you must resort to searching for the animal. But this should not be a random effort. Mark the last point at which you were on the track or blood trail. At that point set up a grid pattern. Use a compass or GPS to keep yourself on course. Search 100 yards to one side of the trail, advance 20 yards or so, and search 100 yards back to the other side of the trail. Closely inspect any brushy pockets, and look behind all logs or other cover. If you're searching with a partner, stay close enough together that you can

see each other. If there are any water sources within or near your search area, look them over closely. An animal that has lost a lot of blood will be thirsty and will seek water, and it could be feverish and lie down in the water. A logical, systematic search like this often will lead to the recovery of animals that have left no clearly defined trail.

*Summary:* If you wait for the right moment to shoot, carefully select your aiming point, and shoot straight, you should get a double-lung or heart hit, and you will find your animal less than 100 yards from the point where it was hit. That's the ideal scenario, and that will describe 90 percent of your opportunities at animals if you follow the procedures described in this chapter.

On occasion, however, things will not go as perfectly as planned, and you could end up with a trailing job. That just adds to the challenge of the hunt. If you approach the trail with the attitude that you are going to search until you find your animal, and you apply the trailing techniques described here, you can count on a celebration at the end of the trail.

*Often, the only blood left by an animal will be smearing from its fur onto the undersides of leaves and grass. You will never see this blood by looking down from above. You must get down on the ground and look up under the vegetation, as Larry D. Jones is doing here.*

*Chapter 10*

# In the End

Up to this point, I have emphasized primarily equipment and how-to, both essential tools for successful bowhunting. But as in any other sport or activity, tools in bowhunting are only as good as the brain behind them. In that sense, your mind may be your most important hunting tool.

After all, anyone with adequate time, money, and effort can acquire the equipment and physical skills needed for bowhunting. Many people do that. Yet many of these people never become good bowhunters, because they never learn to think like bowhunters.

To put it another way, a bowhunter is not just a gun hunter with a bow in his hand. He's a whole different creature, and hunting successfully with a bow demands a special mindset. Notice that some people take to bowhunting right away; it just comes naturally for them. Others seem never to get the hang of it. I personally know several such people. They have the knowledge, the physical ability, and the best equipment. Yet after years of bowhunting, they just can't quite make it work, because they still don't think like bowhunters. They're simply rifle hunters with bows in their hands.

*A bowhunter is not just a rifle hunter with a bow in his hand. He is a whole new creation with a unique mindset.*

What does it mean to think like a bowhunter? And how do you come to that point? Here are some thoughts along this line.

# Getting the Shot

I've heard hunters say something like, "I couldn't get any closer so I had to take a long shot." Had to take a shot? You never have to take a shot. The whole idea in bowhunting is to get close to animals. That's what makes bowhunting unique and gives it special thrill.

But more to the point, the goal in bowhunting — any hunting for that matter — is never to get a shot. It's to make a clean kill. And if you have any doubt about your ability to do that in any given situation, then don't release the bowstring. If you're thinking like a bowhunter, you will do everything necessary to put yourself into position to get a high-percentage shot.

A high-percentage shot begins with shooting distance. That is, you have to be within your personal accuracy range. For some, that might be 20 yards, for others maybe 30 or 40. For the very best archers, it could be 50. The discussion here is not to prescribe a maximum shooting distance; that has been done earlier. No, the discussion here is to analyze the bowhunter's mind, which says that you won't shoot — even think about shooting — until you know you're within your effective range. That's the only ethical approach. That's how a bowhunter thinks.

*The goal in bowhunting — any hunting for that matter — is never just to get a shot. It's to make a clean kill. Never release an arrow until you're in position for a high-percentage shot.*

In earlier discussions on shot placement, I also emphasized the need for shooting at calm, unaware animals. If you're 20 yards from a deer, you probably are well within your accuracy range. But if that deer is looking at you, wired, and ready to spring, you do not have a good shot. Again, the discussion here is not on shot selection and placement; it's on attitude, which always should be set on getting a close shot at a calm, undisturbed animal.

If it is, you will develop hunting methods and stealth that ensure getting close without being detected. You will select equipment, clothing, and footwear that allow you to move quietly and without detection, even at close range. You will choose hunting methods, whether hunting from a tree stand or ground blind, by still-hunting or stalking, that work best under the given conditions. You will develop and practice stealth.

My friend Don Pritchett uses the word "flow" to describe the stealth process. "Nothing moves fast in the woods," Pritchett said. "In an undisturbed forest, the atmosphere is quiet and calm, and all the creatures there move slowly. The only thing that moves faster than game is a predator. Deer and elk will spot anything moving fast. There's a certain flow in the woods, and to be consistent in bowhunting you can't break that flow."

Patience and slow movement are probably the essence

of flow, but the concept goes much further. It's a whole mindset. If you're thinking like a bowhunter, you won't just pull on your blue jeans and clodhoppers and go rambling through the woods, hoping to get a shot or two at deer.

People who are satisfied to get within 100 yards and then to start slinging arrows, or who launch arrows at fleeing animals, hoping for a lucky hit, pervert the whole concept of bowhunting. The objects are the thrill of close-range encounters and clean kills. If these aren't your goals, take up another sport. Bowhunting is not for you.

## Making the Shot

Hunting with a rifle in the 1950s and 1960s, my dad killed mule deer every year, and to my knowledge he never missed a deer. He was very good. Yet, between seasons he never took his rifle from the cabinet, never practiced. His gun was sighted in, and he knew how to shoot it. What else mattered? He always killed deer.

I'm neither advocating nor excusing his behavior. My only point is that his approach would not have produced the same results in bowhunting. For at least three reasons, bowhunters must dedicate themselves to regular practice, year around.

One is the intimate nature of the tackle. A bow is literally an extension of your body. You supply the power, and, because you're always shooting off-hand, your conditioning and form are critical to accuracy. You cannot sandbag or rest a bow to make up for deficiencies in shooting skills. To put it another way, your body is part of your shooting equipment, and it must be kept in tune right along with your bow.

Additionally, a bow can change point of impact during inactivity. The string (and cables on a compound) can creep, and after six months in a closet, the arrows may be hitting off target, even if the bow has not been touched. The only way to keep your bow — and your body — tuned is practice, practice, practice.

Finally, shooting proficiency must be ingrained. You must practice enough that you essentially go on autopilot when you draw, aim, and release an arrow. That's because getting close to animals affects your mind far differently from shooting animals at long range. The bowhunter who can draw on an animal at 20 yards, while staying focused and cool, is rare. Most of us cannot. We start quaking and fretting, our hearts pound, our minds go blank. We're a mess. That's why we must practice regularly. We must ingrain good shooting habits into our minds and bodies, so that under the stress of buck fever, we will perform flawlessly — despite ourselves. Otherwise, success will be elusive at best.

## Confidence

If hunting and shooting skills are the tools for success, then confidence is the current that powers them. In my early years of bowhunting, I had little confidence. I loved roaming the mountains and packing a bow, but I didn't expect to kill anything, and only shear bullheadedness kept me going. However, with time and a few modest successes, I finally discovered: *Hey, I can do this. I can bowhunt as well as anyone.* With that revelation, my confidence — and my success — rose markedly. Almost magically I became a far better bowhunter, simply because I finally believed in the bow and in myself.

Confidence, and lack thereof are classic self-fulfilling prophecies. Confident people find a way to get the job done. Conversely, doubt-filled people normally find a way to fail. To bowhunt well, you must have confidence in your bow, your techniques — and yourself.

Confidence may be partly genetic. Some people just seem to be born winners, and they exude confidence in everything they do, throughout their lives. They're fortunate.

The rest of us aren't so lucky, and we must develop our own confidence. While that might seem easier said than done, it's far from impossible.

Chuck Adams, who has bow-killed more record book animals than anyone in history, seems to exude confidence. When I asked him why he seemed so confident, he said, "Preparation. My first three years of bowhunting, I did not kill a thing. In fact, I could not envision an arrow going into an animal. And when it finally happened, I was astonished. I had no confidence.

"Now I consider confidence the single biggest factor in my success. Confidence is something you acquire. You earn it. It's at the top of a pyramid with a broad base of successes and preparation below it.

"The reason I'm confident now is that I work so hard the rest of the year, perfecting my gear, working on my shooting. When the season arrives, my bow almost shoots itself, and I know my gear will not let me down. I have no doubts."

Knowledge is another basis for confidence. Back when I started in bowhunting, a person had to dig pretty hard to learn how to bowhunt. Few books and magazines on bowhunting existed; and videos, DVDs, and TV programs about bowhunting were nonexistent. So, many of us went into the field with scant knowledge. No wonder we lacked confidence.

Today, thousands of books, magazines, videos, TV programs, seminars, and Internet websites place infinite knowledge at the fingertips of every bowhunter. You want confidence? Saturate yourself with the knowledge. You can learn so much simply from research and study, you will feel like a stud bowhunter before you ever enter the field.

In my early years, I had no confidence. But a few modest victories like this buck convinced me I could do this. As my confidence grew, so did my bowhunting success.

Then work on your mind in other ways. The term visualization has been so overworked it has lost much of its potency. Still the concept is valid. Essentially, visualization means you picture yourself performing a feat — hitting a winning tennis stroke, rolling a strike in bowling, making a perfect archery shot — and the winning images imbedded in your subconscious will lead to actual successes. That might seem like pure mental gymnastics, but visualization has proven effective for professional athletes, and I think it has helped my hunting.

Another mental concept is "self-talk." Notice that throughout life you're always talking to yourself — about yourself. What are you saying? "I'm a loser? I never do anything right?" Or, "I can do this. I'm da man!" If your self-talk is all negative, is it any wonder you fail? You're talking yourself into failure. If that's the case, have a little talk with yourself about changing your attitude. Learn to talk positively about yourself. Again, this might seem like so much mental hocus-pocus, but without a doubt you'll perform better if you see yourself as a winner, not a loser. A "can-do" attitude is a fundamental pillar of confidence.

Another is experience. If you've proven to yourself you can do something once, you will have confidence you can do it again. Frankly, I think all the emphasis on trophy bucks and huge bulls these days hurts recruitment of new bowhunters. When magazines, TV programs, Internet sites, and record books emphasize the taking of only mature animals, beginning bowhunters feel guilty for shooting anything less than a record book specimen.

That's hogwash. No one can learn without experience. If you're new to bowhunting, my advice is to shoot the first legal animals you can get within bow range. If those are yearling does or spike bucks, good enough. They will eat great, and with some success behind you, you'll be ready when the big boy shows up. If you're young, you'll have plenty of time for shooting record book animals. First get some experience of bagging animals under your belt. Build your confidence. Then when the giant buck comes along, you'll be able to perform.

Finally, maintain realistic expectations. In many states, bowhunters average less than 5 percent success, and in the best states they rarely exceed 30. Also, they generally average less than half the success rate of gun hunters, and, on average, they spend far more time in the field for each animal killed.

In other words, bowhunters do far more hunting than killing. Bowhunting is a game of what ifs, almosts, if onlys, and close calls. Thus, to last in bowhunting, you must love hunting for the sake of hunting. You must thrive on challenge and learning, on nature observation, on the sight of animals up close — even if you can't shoot them. You must crave the smell of earth and plants, the sight of a sunrise, the feel of rain and wind, the thrill of close calls. These are the essence of bowhunting, and they're all you'll get most of the time. If you can't accept that, then bowhunting will be a tedious and frustrating trial for you. To stick with bowhunting, you must focus on the process, the love of hunting. With your mind fixed there, you'll be a good bowhunter.

## Commitment

Some people accuse hard-core bowhunters of being elitist. They say we're too serious, that we're trying to exclude people. In a sense that's true. I can't speak for anyone, but here's my feeling: I welcome everyone into bowhunting — if they're willing to take it seriously.

You see, it's okay to be a duffer in golf or bowling. Nothing gets hurt except your ego. But it's not all right to be a duffer at bowhunting. In bowhunting, we hold the power of life and death, and that demands the responsibility to wield that power ethically and efficiently.

Not only the lives of animals but the future of bowhunting depend on our commitment. A goofball who brags about "sticking" an animal not only shows disregard for the animal but he taints all bowhunters, because those who hate hunting and would stop it at any cost will inflate any one dark episode to make us all look like hoodlums.

This isn't to say that everyone who touches a bow must commit his entire life to the bow and arrow, only that we all — whether we're weekend bowhunters or hard-core extremists — must be competent and conscientious. Anyone unwilling to reach and maintain a basic level of competence should play somewhere else. For the sake of the animals and the future of bowhunting, all bowhunters must be committed to competence. Anyone who makes that commitment will enjoy a lifetime of bowhunting pleasure and success.

# Index

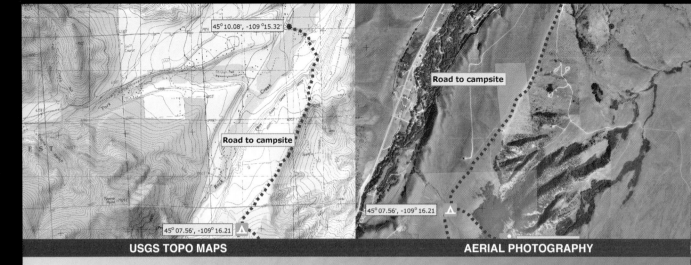